More Making Out in Japanese

Revised Edition

by Todd & Erika Geers
revised by Glen McCabe

TUTTLE PUBLISHING
Tokyo • Rutland, Vermont • Singapore

Glen McCabe would like to thank Hiromi Fumoto, Kazu Wada, Hiroko Irita, Nobu Kanno, Tama Kanayama and Etsuko Sato for their invaluable assistance.

Published by Periplus Editions (HK) Ltd. with editorial offices at 364 Innovation Drive, North Clarendon VT 05759 and 130 Joo Seng Road, #06-01/03 Singapore 368357

LCC Card No. 89-51323
ISBN 0-8048-3345-1
ISBN 4-8053-0713-7 (for sale in Japan only)

Printed in Singapore

Distributed by:

Japan
Tuttle Publishing
Yaekari Building 3F
5-4-12 Osaki, Shinagawa-ku
Tokyo 141-0032, Japan
Tel: (03) 5437 0171 Fax: (03) 5437 0755
Email: tuttle-sales@gol.com

North America, Latin America & Europe
Tuttle Publishing
364 Innovation Drive
North Clarendon, VT 05759-9436, USA
Tel: (802) 773 8930 Fax: (802) 773 6993
Email: info@tuttlepublishing.com
www.tuttlepublishing.com

Asia-Pacific
Berkeley Books Pte Ltd
130 Joo Seng Road, 06-01/03
Singapore 368357
Tel: (65) 6280 1330 Fax: (65) 6280 6290
Email: inquiries@periplus.com.sg
www.periplus.com

09 08 07 06
7 6 5 4

Contents

Introduction

So no one understands your Japanese? Worse yet, you don't understand theirs. You've planned your Saturday night, spent a week studying one phrase, and you can't wait to use it. You're at a club, armed with the latest edition of Learn Japanese in 27-and-a-1/2-Minutes-a-Day for moral support, and you lay the phrase on that good-looking local. What happens? The response isn't like in the book. Why?

Basically, because the Japanese don't play by the book when it comes to their daily language, just as Westerners don't. So what can you do? Well, you could give up and decimate your chances of getting with anybody, or you could learn to speak real Japanese.

Just as we speak in a relaxed, colloquial manner, so do the Japanese. On trains, in bars, during ball games, or when getting intimate with their partners, they all use shortcuts—it's only natural! If you want to talk the way the Japanese do, then you need to know what to say, how to say it, and when to say it.

And better still, you'll need to know the cultural context it all happens in. We've built in lots of little morsels to help you paint a picture of the real Japan as you go along—this book will be your roadmap on the path to love and satisfaction in Japan! Right then? Okay, let's go!

INFORMATION

It's tricky to teach the proper pronunciation of a foreign language in a book, so we're not going to try, hoping you've already got the basics. To help you out, though, we've joined two and sometimes three or four words together, to make compound words or phrases that are easier to pronounce. Most of them are hyphenated to highlight merged words, to emphasize the slang suffixes and particles, and to facilitate pronunciation and memorization.

For example, the components of **fuzakenaide-yo** （ふざけない でよ）are: **fuzake** (from **fuzakeru**), **naide** (command form of **arimasen**), and the (quite forceful) suffix **-yo.** We've written the compound phrase **fuzakenaide-yo** so that you won't pause while pronouncing it, but say it entirely in one breath; a pause would weaken the impact.

We're sure that you're familiar with the polite question forms **des-ka** ですか and **mas-ka** ますか. Forget them. Except for a few needed for talking to strangers, requesting services, etc., the rest have been dismissed. In informal speech, rising intonation takes the place of these forms. Thus, the final syllables of all words and phrases in this book ending with a question mark should be pronounced with the kind of rising intonation you give to the question "Right?"

Slang that is too faddish is not included in this book, because it comes and goes too quickly. If you use old slang, the reaction of your Japanese date will likely be, "He thinks he's being cool but nobody says that anymore. Hah, hah!" So we've avoided hot slang—if it's out of date people will think that you're funny or square. But feel free to use what you pick up on the street.

VARIATIONS

The terms "boy" and "girl" are used throughout the book, but we're definitely referring to the post-puberty phase here. To eliminate the embarrassing problem of boys using girls' words or vice versa, we've indicated words suitable for use by girls and boys with the symbols ♀ and ♂ respectively. Words and phrases not marked can be used by both sexes, and (b→g) means a boy should use it when talking to a girl. For example:

Don't be upset.	***Okoranaide***. ♀
	怒らないで。
	Okoruna-yo. ♂
	怒るなよ。
Make me warm.	***Atatamete***.
	暖めて。
You look beautiful.	***Kirei-dayo***. (b→g)
	きれいだよ。

But before you go thinking that boys' and girls' speech patterns are absolutely divided, stop a minute. Don't be shocked if you hear a girl using a quite masculine phrase (or vice versa). The gender gap in Japanese speech is narrowing, especially among young people, and there's nothing wrong with "borrowing" for impact or emphasis. We've made the distinction as a general guide to usage.

One thing you'll notice as you speak with the Japanese (especially if you move around) is that people's speech patterns vary wildly. We're not just talking about slang here, there are also big differences between regions and social groups. It's impossible for us to include all the variations (more on the regional ones later) of the phrases in this book, so we've gone with a standard Japanese (***hyōjungo*** 標準語) style, which everyone will understand and which you can adapt to the area you're living in.

Adaptation is really important—the phrases here might seem too harsh to some ears and too soft to others. Take your cues from the speech and reactions of people around you. If they warm up to the way you're talking, great, otherwise think about the way they're taking it and adjust. If all else fails, ask—foreigners aren't expected to know everything!

JAPANESE–ENGLISH–JAPANESE

You'll have seen above that we've written Japanese phrases in two ways—in **Rōmaji** (ローマ字–Western script, with lines above some vowels meaning long sounds) and in Japanese script with **furigana** (phonetic **hiragana** 平仮名 above the Chinese **kanji** 漢字) for an added challenge as you get better. But many phrases are written in another phonetic alphabet, **katakana** 片仮名. **Katakana** are mostly used for foreign words, and there are many of them in this book —for example, "batteries" are *batterii* バッテリー. Among other things, they're also used to write a few Japanese superlatives, such as *chō* チョー (amazing-ly/fantastic-ally).

When using **katakana**, life gets a bit tricky when you hit the limitations of the Japanese language. It has only one final consonant "n," so when the Japanese pronounce English words with other consonant endings, they have to tack on a vowel, usually a "u." "Game" becomes *gēmu* ゲーム, "bed" becomes *beddo* ベッド, etc. With no final r sound, they usually use a long *a*—for example locker becomes *rokkā* ロッカー. And since there is no l sound at all, r is used instead.

There are few sounds that the Japanese can pronounce, so they've created new ways of writing them. A "we" (as in "web") is written ウェ, and v sounds are written as ヴ followed by a **katakana** vowel, as in *va* ヴァ, *vi* ヴィ etc.—though the ability to pronounce the v varies greatly, especially between generations!

The Japanese enjoy scattering English words in their speech and you should do the same. With a little practice, it's easy to get the hang of how to "katakana-ize" an English word, that is, to pronounce it the way a Japanese would, strange as it might seem at first. As a foreigner, you'd be expected to use **katakana** words—so don't hold back!

As a reference point, here's a chart of the 45 **kana** in each alphabet, with the **hiragana** listed first under each sound. There are various ways of writing some **kana** in **Rōmaji** (e.g. *tu* or *tsu*)—we've gone with those closest to the sound.

a あ ア	i いイ	u うウ	e えエ	o おオ
ka かカ	ki きキ	ku くク	ke けケ	ko こコ
ga がガ	gi ぎギ	gu ぐグ	ge げゲ	go ごゴ
sa さサ	shi しシ	su すス	se せセ	so そソ
za ざザ	ji じジ	zu ずズ	ze ぜゼ	zo ぞゾ
ta たタ	chi ちチ	tsu つツ	te てテ	to とト
da だダ	ji ぢヂ	zu づヅ	de でデ	do どド
na なナ	ni にニ	nu ぬヌ	ne ねネ	no のノ
ha はハ	hi ひヒ	fu ふフ	he へヘ	ho ほホ
ba ばバ	bi びビ	bu ぶブ	be べベ	bo ぼボ
pa ぱパ	pi ぴピ	pu ぷプ	pe ぺペ	po ぽポ
ma まマ	mi みミ	mu むム	me めメ	mo もモ
ya やヤ		yu ゆユ		yo よヨ
ra らラ	ri りリ	ru るル	re れレ	ro ろロ
wa わワ				o をヲ
va ヴァ	v ヴィ	vu ヴ	ve ヴェ	vo ヴォ

There are a few more variations to watch out for. Notables are the use of *ha* as the subject particle, in which case it's read *wa* (such as *watashi-wa* 私は), and verbs ending in -masu ます, which we've romanised to *-mas*, because that's how you say it. You'll pick them up as you go along.

BEING CHOOSY

There are plenty of phrases for which the Japanese have alternatives, as in any language. We've listed the phrases in a rough order from least to most casual, also getting more vulgar as they become more casual. If what you're saying doesn't seem to fit the mood, again, adapt to the speech of the people around you!

In the book, we've included the Japanese words for "me" and "you" in many phrases. In practice, they are often left out, unless particular clarification is needed, but until you can instinctively understand who is being referred to, it's best to use them. If you do, there are a range of words available, not just the gender-neutral *watashi* 私 (with its super-formal counterpart *watakushi* 私) and *anata* あなた that textbooks love.

For girls, there's *atashi* あたし, and for guys there's *boku* 僕 and *ore* 俺. To say "you," girls can say *anata* あなた or *anta* あんた, and guys can say *kimi* 君 or *omae* お前. In this book, we've stuck with *anata* and *kimi*, because these are the "safest" for everyday conversation. *Omae* and *ore* in particular are very harsh, and can put people off. Until you know when best to use these words (again judge by the speech of the Japanese around you), steer clear!

STRESSED OUT OVER ENDINGS

One thing that we have to say is that in Japanese, how you say something can have more meaning that what you say. Think about it: when you're sharing an intimate moment, you can convey many emotions by sounding caring and serious, on top of what you're actually saying. Some phrases can be changed from statements to questions just by the tone or particle at the end... the list goes on. Here's a run-down of some slang endings and tonal tricks.

For starters, the rules say that plain negative verbs end in **-nai** (e.g. **wakaranai** 分からない I don't understand/know). But you'll hear other forms, like **-n**, as in **wakaran** 分からん, or **shiran** 知らん (I dunno) or special corruptions like **wakannai** 分かんない and **iu** 言う pronounced **yū** ゆう. (Plain positive forms generally don't change as they're pretty simple already).

The most common slang final particle is **ne,** often lengthened to **nē**. Only partly fictitious, it seems to us that when a new-born Japanese baby is shown off for the first time, someone will say **Kawaii-nē?** かわいいねえ？ (Isn't he/she cute?), and inevitably the flock of admirers will all say **Nē!** ねえ！ (Oh yes!). From such early exposure, the child is doomed to utter **nē** for the rest of his/her life.

Nē gives a familiar yet emphatic ending, usually to rhetorical questions, and lengthening it adds more emphasis. With a falling intonation it's more of an explanation. It isn't often said with a rising intonation, but can be said in a high pitch for emphasis. Girls prefer **ne** and **nē,** and guys have an alternative, **na**, which is used in the same way. But as we said before, the gender (speech) gap is narrowing, especially around women, guys will often use **ne.**

Other handy sentence endings include **yo** よ, used to empha-sise that "I'm telling you what I think (and you should do this)." **Wa** わ is often added by women to soften phrases, and you'll see it throughout this book. If you prefer a more blunt style, don't use it, or use **yo** instead. **-noda** 〜のだ (less formally **-nda** 〜んだ) makes the sentence a clear explanation, with a feeling of "that's the way it is."

These can be combined liberally. For example, you're trying to decide which movie to see, and someone is being quite pushy about their choice. To be clear that you've already seen it and once was enough, you can say **Mō mitan-dayone** もう見たんだよね。

Zo ぞ and **ze** ぜ can be added (usually by guys) to give instructions. **Zo** means "let's do..." as in **Yoshi, iku-zo** よし、行くぞ (Right, let's go), similar to but slightly harsher than **ikō** 行こう. **Ze** is a very strong command form, e.g. **Iku-ze!** 行くぜ！ (Move it!) Finally, **-kke** is a handy ending, expressing either uncertainty or forgetfulness **Nan-datta-kke?** 何だったっけ？ (What was it again...?)

The meaning of some phrases may be changed from a statement to a question by a rising final intonation, and these phrases are marked by diamonds (◆). For example:

Haven't seen you around for a while.	◆**Hisashiburi-ne.** ♀ 久しぶりね。 ◆**Hisashiburi-dane.** 久しぶりだね。

With a rising intonation, the sentence becomes "Haven't seen you around for a while, have I?"

And which parts of the phrase you stress also make a big difference—stressing a **yo** emphasizes that you're pushing your opinion. Stressing the **sō** in **sō-dane/sō desu-ne** そうだね/そうですね (that's right) means you agree more strongly.

Finally, put emotion into your voice. You might think that the Japanese spoken around you is emotionless because it seems so fast, but nothing could be further from the truth. Put feeling into your voice as you would in English, and your message will be loud and clear.

THE LAST WORD

Does all of this sound really daunting? It shouldn't! Think of this introduction as a reference page for your journey through the Japanese-speaking world. Just keep these points in mind, and you'll find this book a valuable resource to speed your street-Japanese skills along.

And there's one last thing: the Japanese love to see foreigners making an effort to speak Japanese! Through their troubles learning English, they know how hard it is, so even if you can't get the point across to start with, keep trying and you'll earn more respect. And if you're using real phrases like the ones in this book, all the better!

Getting to Know You

1

Hello! Hi!

Ohayō!
おはよう！
Konnichi-wa!
こんにちは！
Komban-wa!
こんばんは！

Ohayō! is used in the morning, say until 10A.M., and with people you're seeing for the first time that day. *Konnichi-wa!* is for the daytime, and *Komban-wa!* for the evening.

As everyday phrases, there are many variations and contractions of these, formal and informal, and they differ between regions of Japan—but these are the universal standards!

Hajimemashite
はじめまして。

This is a (somewhat formal) word you use to say hi to someone you haven't met before.

Allow us to introduce ourselves.	*Atashitachi-no jikoshōkai-sasete.* ♀ あたしたちの自己紹介させて。 *Bokutachi-no jikoshōkai-sasete.* ♂ 僕たちの自己紹介させて。
Would you introduce your friends?	*Anata-no tomodachi-o shōkai-shite?* ♀ あなたの友達を紹介して？ *Kimi-no tomodachi-o shōkai-shite?* ♂ 君の友達を紹介して？
I'm...	*Atashi-wa...* ♀ あたしは... *Boku-wa...* ♂ 僕は...

This is usually your first chance to practice katakana-ized pronunciation. It's sometimes a good idea to say your name in its original pronunciation first, and then in **katakana** form, which lets your new friend choose whether to try the "foreign version" or play safe with **katakana**—a choice they'll appreciate.

Where do you live?	*Doko-ni sunderu-no?* どこに住んでるの？
Where do you come from?	*Dokkara kita-no?* どっから来たの？

Doko-ni sunderu-no? should be used if you are introduced by someone. If there is no introduction, both *Doko-ni sunderu-no?* and *Dokkara kita-no?* are okay and both produce the same answer. Girls might tell you their address, or they may just say *acchi* あっち, meaning "over there."

I'm from America/ the U.K./Australia/ New Zealand.	*Atashi-wa Amerika/Igirisu/ Ōsutoraria/Nyūjīrando-kara kita.* ♀

あたしはアメリカ/イギリス/
　　オーストラリア/ニュージー
　　ランドから来た。

***Boku-wa Amerika/Igirisu/
Ōsutoraria/Nyūjīrando-kara
kita.*** ♂

僕はアメリカ/イギリス/
　　オーストラリア/ニュージー
　　ランドから来た。

The Japanese don't have a word for Britain—***Igirisu*** is it, and the distinction between England, Great Britain and the U.K. is usually lost on the Japanese. Those wanting to emphasise their Scottish or Welsh background can substitute ***Sukottorando*** スコットランド or ***Uēruzu*** ウェールズ.

| How old are you? | ***Nansai?*** |
| | 何歳？ |

To this question, girls will usually answer with ***Atete!, Nansai-da-to omou?*** あてて！何歳だと思う？ "Guess! How old do you think I am?," or ***Ikutsu-ni mieru?*** いくつに見える？ "How old do I look?"

Are you an only child?	***Anata-hitorikko?*** ♀
	あなた一人っ子？
	Kimi hitorikko? ♂
	君一人っ子？

Are you the oldest?	***Anata ichiban ue?*** ♀
	あなた1番上？
	Kimi ichiban ue? ♂
	君1番上？

| Are you a student? | ***Gakusei?*** |
| | 学生？ |

The answer might be ***kōkōsei*** (high school student) 高校生 ***daigakusei*** 大学生 (university student), ***sen-mon-gakkōsei*** 専門学校生 (student of a specialist school–e.g. dental assistant, nurse...), ***tandaisei*** 短大生 (junior/two-year college student, almost all of whom are women).

What type of school?

Donna gakkō?
どんな学校？

I went to a regular/ special (trade) school.

Atashi-wa futsū-no/senmon gakkō-ni itta. ♀
あたしは普通の／専門学校に
行った。

Boku-wa futsū-no/senmon gakkō-ni itta. ♂
僕は普通の／専門学校に行った。

Where are you studying? (i.e. at what institution)

Doko-de benkyō shiteru-no?
どこで勉強してるの？

What do (did) you study at the university?

Daigaku-de nani-o senkō- shiteru (shita)-no?
大学で何を専攻してる(した)の？

Senkō means "major study area."

I did economics/law/ politics/English/ Spanish.

Keizai/Hōritsu/Seiji/Eigo/ Supeingo-o benkyō shita.
経済／法律／政治／英語／
スペイン語を勉強した。

What's your job?

Shigoto nani shiten-no?
仕事何してんの？

How do you spend your time?

Itsumo nani shiten-no?
いつも何してんの？

Will you be my Japanese teacher?	*Atashi-ni nihongo-o oshiete-kureru?* ♀ あたしに日本語を教えてくれる？ *Boku-ni nihongo-o oshiete-kureru?* ♂ 僕に日本語を教えてくれる？
I'll teach you English.	*Atashi-ga eigo-o oshiete ageru.* ♀ あたしが英語を教えてあげる。 *Boku-ga eigo-o oshiete ageru.* ♂ 僕が英語を教えてあげる。

Pithy as these sound to Western ears, the Japanese often say things like this and like to hear them—even if they're only a prelude to more conversation!

Have I seen you before?	*Mae-ni (atta-koto) attakke?* 前に（会ったこと）あったっけ？ *Mae-ni atta-koto nai?* 前に会ったことない？
You come here often, don't you?	*Koko-ni yoku kuru-yone?* ここによく来るよね？
I've been watching you.	*Anata-no-koto zutto mitetano-yo.* ♀ あなたのことずっと見てたのよ。 *Kimi-no-koto zutto mitetan dayo.* ♂ 君のことずっと見てたんだよ。

It's better to soften these two phrases into "semi-questions" by using a rising intonation.

You're really pretty.	*Kimi-tte hontō-ni kawaii-ne.* ♂ 君って本当にかわいいね。
You're handsome.	*Anata-tte sugoku kakkoii-ne.* ♀ あなたってすごくかっこいいね。 *Suteki da-ne.* ♂ すてきだね。

You're fascinating.	*Anata-wa miryokuteki-ne.* ♀
	あなたは魅力的ね。
	Kimi-tte miryokuteki-dane. ♂
	君って魅力的だね。
I want to know more about you.	*Anata-to motto hanashitai* ♀
	あなたともっと話したい。
	Kimi-to motto hanashitai ♂
	君ともっと話したい。

Though this literally means "I want to talk with you more," it's softer than the phrases below, and so is more suited to someone you've only met recently.

	Anata-no-koto motto shiritai. ♀
	あなたのこともっと知りたい。
	Kimi-no-koto motto shiritai. ♂
	君のこともっと知りたい。
Come on, tell me more.	*Ī-janai. Motto oshiete-yo.*
	いいじゃない。もっと教えてよ。
You don't talk very much.	*Anata-wa ammari shaberanai-none.* ♀
	あなたはあんまりしゃべらないのね。
	Kimi-wa ammari shaberanai-ne. ♂
	君はあんまりしゃべらないね。
Don't be shy.	*Hazukashigaranaide.*
	恥ずかしがらないで。

Also means "Don't be embarrassed."

Ask me some questions.	*Nanka kiite.*
	何か聞いて。
Ask me anything you want.	*Nandemo kiite-ii-yo.*
	何でも聞いていいよ。
Except what color underwear I'm wearing.	*Nani iro-no shitagi-o tsuketeruka-wa oshienai kedo.*
	何色の下着をつけてるかは教えないけど。

I like your personality.	*Anata-no seikaku suki-yo.* ♀ あなたの性格好きよ。 *Kimi-no seikaku suki-dayo.* ♂ 君の性格好きだよ。
You're my type.	*Anata-wa atashi-no-suki-na* 　　　*taipu.* ♀ あなたはあたしの好きなタイプ。 *Kimi-wa boku-no suki-na* 　　　*taipu.* ♂ 君は僕の好きなタイプ。 *Kimi-wa boku-no konomi.* ♂ 君は僕の好み。
What kind of people 　do you like?	*Donna hito-ga suki?* どんな人が好き？ *Donna hito-ga taipu?* どんな人がタイプ？

You can substitute the subsequent words into the following sentence:

I like...type of person.	...*hito-ga ii.* …人がいい

quiet: *otonashii* おとなしい
　mukuchi-na 無口な

loud: *nigiyaka-na* にぎやかな

tender: *yasashii* 優しい

funny: *omoshiroi* 面白い

tough: *tafu-na* タフな

serious/dedicated:
　majime-na 真面目な

considerate: *omoiyari-no aru*
　　　思いやりのある

cheerful: *genki-na (-no aru)*
　　　元気な(のある)

rich: *okane-mochi-no*
　　　お金持ちの

stylish: *sutairisshu-na*
　　　スタイリッシュな

shy: *hazukashigari-ya-na*
　　　恥ずかしがりな

bright: *akarui* 明るい

elite: *erīto-na* エリートな

manly: *otokoppoi*
　　　男っぽい

feminine: *onnappoi*
　　　女っぽい

outgoing: *shakoteki-na*
　　　社交的な

smart: *atama-no ii*
　　　頭のいい

glamorous: *guramā-na*
　　　グラマーな

chubby: *potchari-shita*
　　　ぽっちゃりした

slim: *yaseteru* やせてる

thin-waisted: *uesto-ga hosoi* ウエストが細い

big: *ōkii* 大きい

big eyes: *me-ga ōkii* 目が大きい

small: *chīsai* 小さい

small butt: *chīsai oshiri-no* 小さいおしりの

small breasts: *mune-no chīsai* 胸の小さい

small mouth: *kuchi-no chīsai* 口の小さい

long hair: *kami-no nagai* 髪の長い

long legs: *ashi-no nagai* 足の長い

pretty teeth: *ha-no kirei-na* 歯のきれいな

cute: *kawaii* かわいい

cute smile: *egao-no kawaii* 笑顔のかわいい

sexy: *sekushī-na* セクシーな

sporty: *supōtī-na* スポーティな

I like your hairstyle.	*Anata-no heasutairu ga suki.* ♀ あなたのヘアスタイルが好き *Kimi-no heasutairu ga suki.* ♂ 君のヘアスタイルが好き
Do you follow the latest fads?	*Ryūkō-o ou?* 流行を追う？
What's popular now?	*Ima nani-ga hayatteru-no?* 今何がはやってるの？

You have good taste in
clothes.

Fuku-no sensu-ga ii-ne.
服のセンスがいいね。
Fuku no sensu-ga ii-na. ♂
服のセンスがいいな。

I'm not very stylish.

*Atashi-wa ammari sutairisshu/
oshare-janai.* ♀
あたしはあんまりスタイリッシュ／
おしゃれじゃない。
*Boku-wa ammari ssutairisshu/
oshare-janai.* ♂
僕はあんまりスタイリッシュ／
おしゃれじゃない。

Said especially of clothes.

Will you give me some
advice?

Nanika adobaisu-shite-kureru?
何かアドバイスしてくれる？

Shall we go shopping
together someday?

*Kondo issho-ni shoppingu-ni
ikanai?*
今度一緒にショッピングに
行かない？

I don't like to shop alone.

*Hitori-de shoppingu-suru-no-
wa suki-janai.*
ひとりでショッピングするのは
好きじゃない。

Do you have a steady
boy/girlfriend?

Tsukiatteru hito iru?
付き合ってる人いる？

You must be very
popular.

Moteru-deshō.
もてるでしょう。
Moteru-darō. ♂
もてるだろう。

You must have many
girlfriends/boyfriends.
(You must be popular.)

Kanojo ippai irun-deshō. ♀
彼女いっぱいいるんでしょう。
Kareshi ippai irun-darō. ♂
彼氏いっぱいいるんだろう。

You must have a girlfriend.	*Kanojo irun-deshō.* ♀

彼女いるんでしょう。

You must have a boyfriend.	*Kareshi irun-darō.* ♂

彼氏いるんだろう。

The nuance is "You're good-looking, so I think you must have a steady girlfriend/boyfriend." Use these phrases to check if they are available without coming right out and asking!

Yes, I had one, but we have just broken up.	*Un, demo, saikin wakareta.*

うん、でも、最近別かれた。

I've never dated a Japanese boy/girl before.	*Nihonjin-no otoko-to dēto-shita-koto-nai.* ♀

日本人の男とデートしたことない。

Nihonjin-no onna-to dēto-shita-koto-nai. ♂

日本人の女とデートしたことない。

Will you go out with me?	*Atashi-to dekakenai?* ♀

あたしと出かけない？

Boku-to dekakenai? ♂

僕と出かけない？

Do you believe in destiny?	*Unmei-tte shinjiru?*

運命って信じる？

If I hadn't taken that train/gone to that bar, we wouldn't have met.	*Ano densha-ni noranakattara/ ano bā-ni ikanakattara atashitachi awanakattan-dane.* ♀

あの電車に乗らなかったら／
あのバーに行かなかったら
あたしたち会わなかったん
だね。

Ano densha-ni noranakattara/ ano bā-ni ikanakattara bokutachi awanakattan-dane. ♀

あの電車に乗らなかったら／
あのバーに行かなかったら
僕たち会わなかったんだね。

Let's do this again. *Mata kore shiyō.*
またこれしよう。

Let's get together later. *Ato-de mata-ne.*
後でまたね。

This means "Let's separate now and get back together later (today)."

Let's see each other again. *Mata aō.*
また会おう。

Let's meet on Tuesday at *Kayōbi-ni anata-no okiniiri-no*
your favorite café. *kafe-de aō.* ♀
火曜日にあなたのお気に入りの
カフェで会おう。

Kayōbi-ni kimi-no okiniiri-no
kafe-de aō. ♂
火曜日に君のお気に入りのカフェ
で会おう。

I'm glad we met. *Aete yokatta.*
会えてよかった。

It'd be great to see you *Mata aeruto ureshī.*
again. また会えるとうれしい。

Let's go cheer on our team! | *Hiiki chiimu-o ōen shiyō!*
贔屓チームを応援しよう！

I've always wanted to go to Kōshien Stadium/the Tōkyō Dome... | *Itsumo Kōshien Kyūjō/Tōkyō Dōmu-ni ikitakatta-kedo...*
いつも甲子園 球場／東京ドームに行きたかったけど...

Kōshien (in Kōbe) is famous throughout Japan (and East Asian baseballing circles) as the home of Japanese baseball.

Go! Go for it! (Good luck!) | *Gambatte!*
頑張って！
Gambare!
頑張れ！

Gambare! is stronger, and is used in any situation (speaking directly to someone who is about to sit a test/play sport, cheering for your favorite team, encouraging runners in a marathon...). *Gambatte* is usually only used when speaking directly to someone.

Who is that (player)? | *Are/Ano senshu dare?*
あれ／あの選手だれ？

Let's watch a movie. | *Eiga-o miyō-yo.*
映画を見ようよ。

Who is your favorite actor/actress? | *Yūmeijin-de dare-ga suki?*
有名人で誰が好き？

Yūmeijin means "a famous person," so this is a broadly useful phrase.

Did you see...? ...mita?
...見た？

I saw (it). Mita-mita.
見た見た（！）

This is a (usually feminine) emphatic form, which normally shows enthusiasm.

Mita.
見た。

Mita-yo.
見たよ。

I didn't see (it). *Minakatta.*
見なかった。

I couldn't see (it). *Mienakatta.*
見えなかった。

When you can't see something because something else is in the way, or because you didn't have the chance to go to the movies.

Mi(ra)renakatta.
見（ら）れなかった。

When you can't see something because of your own lack of vision or perception.

I don't want to see (it). *Mitakunai.*
見たくない。

Do you want to see...? *Mitai?*
見たい？

Shall we go and watch it? *Mite miyō-ka?*
見てみようか。

This is of course a good phrase when thinking about movies.

What time does the next *Tsugi-no wa nanji (des-ka)?*
[movie, game etc.] 次のは何時（ですか）。
start?

It's better to add *des-ka* when talking to the likes of shop-keepers and ticket sellers—using casual language may make them less helpful.

We have plenty of time.	***Jikan-ga takusan aru.***
	時間がたくさんある。
	Jikan-ga ippai aru.
	時間がいっぱいある。

The movies in Japan are quite expensive, and with most theaters downtown, are not such a popular option for people in the suburbs. With the proliferation of home theater systems, many people now rent movies instead.

Shall we get a video/ DVD (instead)?	***(Sono kawari) Bideo/DVD-o karate miyō-ka?***
	(その代わり) ビデオ／DVDを借りて見ようか。
Do you know a good place (near here)?	***(Kono hen-no) ii tokoro wakaru?***
	(この辺の）いい所分る？
I know (a good place).	***(Ii tokoro) wakaru(-yo).***
	（いい所）分かる(よ)。

There are of course plenty of other socializing opportunities, with perhaps the most common being ***karaoke***, shopping and relaxing at parks. Of course, there's also the option of clubbing, eating and drinking.

A casual evening or night out in Japan will often involve ***karaoke***. ***Karaoke*** literally means "without orchestra," and this popular activity usually takes place in special ***karaoke*** bars, found throughout cities especially at major railway stations and entertainment areas. The "bars" are collections of many rooms, where you can sing, eat and drink in relative privacy.

The Japanese take their leisure very seriously.

Do you like karaoke?   *Karaoke suki?*
カラオケ好き？

Let's sing karaoke.   *Karaoke utaō/ikō.*
カラオケ歌おう／行こう。

What shall we sing first?   *Mazu-wa nani-ni shiyō-ka.*
まずは何にしようか。

You choose the first song   *(Saki-ni) dōzo.*
  (You go first).   （先に）どうぞ。

This phrase can be used in a variety of situations, from allowing someone to pass through first to letting them pay before you at the cashier. It is of course a sign of good manners and a good way to kick off any communal activity.

Are there any English   *Eigo-no uta aru?*
  songs?   英語の歌ある？

I don't know how to   *Irekata wakaranai.*
  work the machine.   入れ方分からない。

That person's/John's   *Ano ko/hito/Jon-no utaikata*
  singing is funny/   *omoshiroi.*
  interesting.   あの子／人／ジョンの歌い方
          面白い。

Shall we sing something   *Issho-ni utaō-ka?*
  together?   一緒に歌おうか。

Your singing is really good.	***(Uta) jōzu-dane.*** (歌)上手だね。 ***(Uta) umai-ne.*** (歌)うまいね。

It's important to compliment the efforts of others, expecially when they are really good, but you'll also likely be complimented yourself—especially if you try singing in Japanese! A hurried and embarrassed denial (***iie, iie*** いいえ、いいえ) or thank you (***Aa, dōmo*** ああ、どうも) are good ways to reply.

Shall we go shopping?	***Shoppingu-ni ikō-ka.*** ショッピングに行こうか。
Let's go (shopping in) Ginza/Umeda.	***Ginza/Umeda-de shoppingu shiyō.*** 銀座／梅田でショッピングしよう。
I want to go shopping for clothes.	***Yōfuku-o kaitai.*** 洋服を買いたい。
Let's go to Yamashita Park.	***Yamashita Kōen-e ikō.*** 山下公園へ行こう。
I hear it's a good spot for a date.	***Dēto-spotto-datte kiita.*** デートスポットだって聞いた。
Let's go to the park again.	***Mata kōen-ni ikō.*** また公園に行こう。

I love to hold your hand as we walk through the park.	*Anata-to te-o tsunaide kōen-o aruku-noga suki.* ♀ あなたと手をつないで公園を歩くのが好き。 *Kimi-to te-o tsunaide kōen-o aruku-noga suki.* ♂ 君と手をつないで公園を歩くのが好き。
I came here by car.	*Kuruma-de kita.* 車で来た。
Would you like to go for a drive?	*Doraibu-ni ikitai?* ドライブに行きたい？
I have room for two more of your friends.	*Anata-no tomodachi futari-bun-no seki-mo aru-yo.* ♀ あなたの友達二人分の席もあるよ。 *Kimi-no tomodachi futari-bun-no seki-mo aru-yo.* ♂ 君の友達二人分の席もあるよ。

Eating and
Drinking

Would you like something to eat/drink?	*Nanika taberu/nomu?* 何か食べる？／飲む？
Let's get some food.	*Nanika tabeyō.* 何か食べよう。

A general invitiation to get some food, at a buffet or à la carte.

Tabemono tanomō.
食べ物頼もう。

When inviting someone to order food.

The menu, please.	*Menyū-o kudasai.* メニューをください。
What do you want?	*Nani-ga ii?* 何がいい？
Have you decided?	*Kimeta?* 決めた？
I can't decide what to eat.	*Nani tabete ii-ka wakaranai.* 何食べていいか分らない。
I'll order (for us).	*Atashi-ga ōdā-suru/ shite ageru.* ♀ あたしがオーダーする／してあげる。 *Boku-ga oda-suru/ shite ageru.* ♂ 僕がオーダーする／してあげる。
I'll buy it.	*Atashi-ga kau-yo.* ♀ あたしが買うよ。 *Boku-ga kau-yo.* ♂ 僕が買うよ。

This has the connotation of "I'll hand over the money, but we're (probably) paying our own shares."

Gochisō-suru/ogoru-wa. ♀
ごちそうする／おごるわ。
Gochisō-suru/ogoru-yo. ♂
ごちそうする／おごるよ。

This means "I'm paying for yours"—literally "let me treat you."

I/You forgot the chopsticks/ *Ohashi/fōku/naifu/supūn*
forks/knives/spoons.   *wasureta.*
お箸／フォーク／ナイフ／
スプーン忘れた。

There are many rules governing the use of chopsticks. You shouldn't pass food from one set of chopsticks to another, because the Japanese place the ashes of their deceased into a funeral urn this way. It's also extremely offensive to stand chopsticks in a bowl of rice, as this is how food is offered to the spirits of the deceased. Plus, chopsticks should never be grasped in the fist as this is how they would be held for use as a weapon, and it is poor manners to lick them.

That said, once mastered, using chopsticks is second nature, and correct technique and etiquette can get you considerable admiration. If you don't know how, get your Japanese friends to teach you!

Try this!   ***(Kore) tabete mite.***
（これ）食べてみて。

What's it called?   ***Nante iu-no?***
何て言うの？

I've never tried...   ***...tabeta kotonai.***
…食べたことない。

What's you favorite   ***Nihon-no tabemono-de,***
Japanese food?   ***nani-ga ichiban suki?***
日本の食べ物で、何が一番好き？

Can you eat nattō/anko?   ***Nattō/anko taberareru?***
納豆／あんこ食べられる？

Nattō is fermented soybeans, which are stringy and foul-smelling. ***Anko*** is the general name for sweet soybean paste, and like ***nattō*** is often unpalatable to foreigners.

Yes, I can.   *Un, tabe(ra)reru(-yo).*
うん、食べ(ら)れる(よ)。

This is less grammatical but more familiar (and sorter!) expression.

No, I can't.   *Uun, tabe(ra)renai*
ううん、食べ(ら)れない。

(That) looks delicious.   *(Are) oishisō.*
(あれ) おいしそう。

It smells good.   *Ii nioi.*
いいにおい。

Give me a bit more.   *Mō sukoshi.*
もう少し。
Mō chotto.
もうちょっと。

Gimme more.   *(Motto) chōdai.*
もっとちょうだい。

Enough.   *Jūbun.*
充分。
Tariru.
足りる。

Enough?   *Tarita?*
足りた？

Not enough.   *Tarinai.*
足りない。

(Sorry,) I can't eat that.

(Sumimasen,) Sore tabe(ra)renai.
（すみません）それ食べ（ら）れない。

Itadakimas!

Itadakimas!
いただきます！

Almost every Japanese says this before eating. The closest English equivalent is "grace," but without its religious meaning (of receiving from the gods). Don't hesitate to say this, and you may even be complimented on your good manners!

What do you think (about this?)

(Kore-ni tsuite) dōmou?
（これについて）どう思う？

Does this taste good?

Kore oishii?
これおいしい？

It tastes good.

Oishii(!)
おいしい（！）

Oishii is a grossly overused word, which can be voiced with the full gamut of emotions, from enthusiasm to indifference (meaning that it may not be good at all!). The Japanese indicate how they feel by the emotion they put into *oishii*. You can add other words, such as *kekkō oishii* 結構おいしい (it's really good, even without much enthusiasm), but just saying *oishii* and meaning it is usually enough.

It's an unusual taste.

Fushigi-na aji-dane.
不思議な味だね。

It's OK/so-so.	***Mā-mā.*** まあまあ。

These two are also polite ways of saying you don't really like something. The following three phrases are also handy, but best left for eating out, where you won't be insulting anyone by criticizing the food!

It's not good.	***Yokunai.*** よくない。
It doesn't taste good.	***Oishikunai.*** おいしくない。
It's awful.	***Mazui.*** まずい。 ***Hidoi.*** ひどい。
I'm full.	***Onaka(-ga) ippai.*** お腹 (が) いっぱい。
Gochisōsama(-deshita)!	***Gochisōsama(-deshita)!*** ごちそうさま (でした) ！

This is the end-of-meal counterpart to ***itadakimas***. It literally means "it was a feast," and is a sign of appreciation.

Do you smoke?	***Tabako sū?*** タバコ吸う？
This is a nonsmoking section.	***Koko-wa kin-en-seki-dayo.*** ここは禁煙席だよ。
Do you drink (alcohol)?	***Osake nomu?*** お酒飲む？
Do you drink beer/saké/ wine/strong liquor?	***Bīru/nihonshu/wain/tsuyoi osake nomu?*** ビール／日本酒／ワイン／ 強いお酒／飲む？

Osake means both "alcohol" and "saké." As a first question, it'll usually mean just "alcohol," but after that, it's better to say ***nihonshu*** which means only "***saké***."

The free drinks are over there.

Furī dorinku-ga asoko ni aru-yo.
フリードリンクがあそこにあるよ。

Can we buy beer here?

Koko-de bīru kaeru?
ここでビール買える？

The drinks here taste terrible!

Koko-no nomimono saiaku!
ここの飲み物最悪！

Koko-no nomimono saiaku-dayo!
ここの飲み物最悪だよ！

This is not very strong.

Kore usui/ammari kokunai/ tsuyokunai.
これ薄い／あんまりこくない／強くない。

They serve weak drinks here.

Koko-no nomimono zenbu usui.
ここの飲み物全部薄い。

Ask for stronger drinks.

Motto koi nomimono-o tanonde.
もっとこい飲み物を頼んで。

The same, but stronger.

Onaji-no-o kokusuru-yō-ni itte.
同じのをこくするように言って。

Telling your friend to order another drink just like you have, only stronger.

Stronger drinks, please.

Motto tsuyoi nomimono-o kudasai.
もっと強い飲み物を下さい。

When ordering the next round of drinks.

Please make this drink stronger.

Kore motto tsuyokushite/ kokushite kudasai.
これもっと強くして／こくして下さい。

When asking the bartender to strengthen a drink you're not happy with.

Drink up!   *Ikki! Ikki!*
イッキ！イッキ！

Ikki! Ikki! is an encouraging cheer which means something like
"Drink it all up without stopping!"

Cheers!   *Kampai!*
乾杯！

Kampai! is said together as everyone clinks their glasses for a
toast. It literally means "dry glass."

Have a drink to catch   *Toriaezu nomō.*
up!   とりあえず飲もう！

I'm getting drunk.   *Yotte-kichatta.* ♀
酔ってきちゃった。
Yopparatte-kichatta. ♀
酔っ払ってきちゃった。
Yotte-kichatta-yo. ♂
酔ってきちゃったよ。

I'm drunk.   *Yotchatta.*
酔っちゃった。
Yopparatchatta.
酔っ払っちゃった。

Let's split the check (bill).   *Warikan-ni shiyō.*
割り勘にしよう。

Let's have one check (bill).	*Denpyō/shiharai-issho-ni shiyō.* 伝票／支払い一緒にしよう。
One check (bill), please.	*Denpyō/shiharai-o hitotsu-ni shite kudasai.* 伝票／支払いをひとつにして 下さい。
Which credit cards do you accept?	*Dono kurejitto kādo-ga tsukae mas-ka?* どのクレジットカードが使え ますか。

You'll find that many (especially small) shops and restaurants in Japan don't take credit cards. This is because Japan is still a mainly cash-based economy. Though ATMs are common (for withdrawing cash and transferring money) in convenience stores, there's little point-of-sale use of cash cards and virtually no checks. People generally use cash for small purchases and bank transfers for larger ones.

I lost my wallet.	*Saifu-o nakushita.* 財布をなくした。 *Osaifu nakushichatta.* お財布なくしちゃった。
I don't have any money.	*Okane-ga nai.* お金がない。
Can I borrow 10,000 yen?	*Ichiman-en kashite-kureru?* 一万円貸してくれる？
I've got a hangover.	*Futsukayoi.* 二日酔い。
I have a splitting headache.	*Atama-ga suggoku itai.* 頭がすっごく痛い。

You drank too much last night, didn't you?

Kinō-wa nomisugita-nē?
昨日は飲み過ぎたねえ？

Kinō-wa nomisugita-nā? ♂
昨日は飲み過ぎたなあ？

Clubbing 4

Let's go to a nightclub.	*Kurabu-ni ikō.* クラブに行こう。
Let's go to your favorite club.	*Anata-no yoku iku kurabu-ni ikō.* ♀ あなたのよく行くクラブに行こう。 *Kimi-no yoku iku kurabu-ni ikō-yo.* ♂ 君のよく行くクラブに行こうよ。

Use *yoku iku* to describe a place you go to often.

I've never been to a club.	*Mada kurabu-ni itta-koto-nai.* まだクラブに行ったことない。

Many seedy places are run by the *yakuza* (Japanese Mob), and they're not to be messed with! Burly bouncers with bad attitudes are a good indicator of a *yakuza* place—until you know how things work, it's safer to stick to mainstream clubs and/or go with Japanese friends!

Is it true Japanese boys dance together?	*Nihon-no otoko-no-hito-tte otokodōshi-de odorutte hontō?* 日本の男の人って男同士で踊るって本当?

How much is the admission?	*Hairu-no ikura kakaruno?* 入るのいくら掛かるの？
Does it include food [and drink]?	*Tabemono-toka zenbu komi?* 食べ物とか全部込み？
Do we need to become members?	*Koko-wa membā-sei nandesuka?* ここはメンバー制なんですか？
Do we get membership cards?	*Menbāshippu/Menbāzu kādo-wa moraemas-ka?* メンバーシップ／メンバーズ カードはもらえますか？

Said to club staff. When talking to friends, use the less formal *moraeru?* もらえる？

Let's make a line. (Let's get in line.)	*Narabō.* 並ぼう。
Are you waiting in line?	*Naranderun desu-ka?* 並んでるんですか。 *Naranderu-no?* 並んでるの？
You wait here.	*Koko-de matte.* ここで待って。
I'll do it.	*Atashi-ga suru-yo.* ♀ あたしがするよ.。 *Boku-ga suru-yo.* ♂ 僕がするよ。
I'm a member.	*Atashi-wa menbā (desu).* ♀ あたしはメンバー（です）。 *Boku-wa menbā (desu).* ♂ 僕はメンバー（です）。
Here are your tickets.	*Hai, chiketto.* はい、チケット。
Are there lockers here?	*Rokkā arimas-ka?* ロッカーありますか。

Rokkā aru?
ロッカーある？

Short-term storage lockers are common in Japan, in clubs and especially in railway stations.

Let's use the lockers.	***Rokkā-(o) tsukaō.*** ロッカー(を)使おう。
Where do you want to sit?	***Doko-ni suwaritai?*** どこに座りたい？
Let's sit close to the dance floor/bar/ band/ restrooms/ exit/ aisle.	***Dansu furoā/bā/bando/toire/ deguchi/tsūro-no chikaku-ni suwarō.*** ダンスフロア／バー／バンド／ トイレ／出口／通路の近くに 座ろう。
It's noisy here.	***Koko urusakunai?*** ここうるさくない？
It's too noisy here.	***Koko urusasugiru-yone.*** ここうるさ過ぎるよね。
There are too many people here.	***Hito-ōi-yone.*** 人多いよね。 ***Konderu-yone.*** こんでるよね。
It's dark over there.	***Mukō/Acchi kurai-yone?*** 向こう／あっち暗いよね？
These seats look good.	***Kono isu ii-yone.*** このいすいいよね。
Let's move to a bigger table.	***Motto ōkii tēburu-ni utsurō.*** もっと大きいテーブルに移ろう。
We need another chair.	***Mō hitotsu isu-ga iru.*** もうひとついすが要る。
I'll get that one over there.	***Are mottekuru.*** あれ持って来る。

I'll bring it with me.	**_Motteku._** 持ってく。
You sit here.	**_Koko-ni suwatte._** ここに座って。
I'll sit here.	**_Koko-ni suwaru._** ここに座る。
Sit by me.	**_Atashi-no soba/yoko-ni suwatte._** ♀ あたしのそば／横に座って。 **_Boku-no soba/yoko-ni suwatte._** ♂ 僕のそば／横に座って。

Soba means "close" and _yoko_ means "beside."

Sit closer.	**_Motto chikaku-ni suwatte._** もっと近くに座って。
If I get drunk, it'll be okay.	**_Moshi atashi-ga yopparatte-mo daijōbu._** ♀ もしあたしが酔っ払っても大丈夫。 **_Moshi boku-ga yopparatte-mo daijōbu._** ♂ もし僕が酔っ払っても大丈夫。
Let's pair off.	**_Pea ni naranai?_** ♀ ペアにならない？ **_Pea ni narōyo._** ♂ ペアになろうよ。

Will you dance with me?   *Atashi-to odotte-kureru?* ♀
あたしと踊ってくれる？
Boku-to odotte-kureru? ♂
僕と踊ってくれる？
Isshoni odoranai?
一緒に踊らない？

I like to watch you dance.   *Anata-no dansu-o miru-noga suki.* ♀
あなたのダンスを見るのが好き。
Kimi-no dansu-o miru-noga suki. ♂
君のダンスを見るのが好き。

I'm not good at dancing.   *Dansu umakunai-no.* ♀
ダンスうまくないの。
Dansu umakunain-da. ♂
ダンスうまくないんだ。

I like slow dancing.   *Surō dansu-ga suki.*
スローダンスが好き。

Are you having fun?   *Tanoshinderu?*
楽しんでる？

Yes!   *Un, tanoshinderu.*
うん、楽しんでる。
Sō-yo! ♀
そうよ！

Not really.   *Ammari.*
あんまり。
Betsu-ni.
別に。

I don't feel like dancing yet.   *Mada odoritakunai.*
まだ踊りたくない。

I'm not going to dance yet.   *Mada odoranai.*
まだ踊らない。

I can't dance to this music.   *Kono kyoku-ja odorenai.*
この曲じゃ踊れない。

I don't know this song.	*Kono uta shiranai.* この歌知らない。
I like rock 'n' roll.	*Rokkun-rōru-ga suki.* ロックンロールが好き。
I like jazz.	*Jazu-ga suki.* ジャズが好き。
I like American Top-40.	*Amerikan toppu-fōtii-no ongaku/kyoku-ga suki.* アメリカントップフォーティーの 音楽／曲が好き。
I like Japanese pop music.	*Jei-poppu ga suki.* ジェイ・ポップが好き。

The dance-floor lights are cool.	*Furoa-no raito kakkoii-ne.* フロアのライトかっこいいね。 *Furoa-no raito kakkoii-na.* ♂ フロアのライトかっこいいな。
Dancing makes me hot.	*Dansu-shitara atsukunatta-yo.* ダンスしたら暑くなったよ。
Hot, as in sweaty.	
Let's get some fresh air.	*Chotto soto ikō.* ちょっと外行こう。
What time do they close?	*Nanji-ni shimaru-no?* 何時に閉まるの？

What time is the last train?　*Saishū densha nanji?*
最終電車何時？

What time do you have　*Nanji-ni shigoto iku-no?*
to be at work?　何時に仕事行くの？

What time is your curfew?　*Mongen nanji?*
門限何時？

We'll never make it.　*Zettai maniawanai.*
絶対間に合わない。

It's already too late.　*Mō osoi.*
もう遅い。

We've got time.　*Jikan-wa aru.*
時間はある。

Let's stay to the end.　*Saigo/owari-made iyō.*
最後／終わりまでいよう。

Let's stay till they throw　*Oidasareru-made iyō.*
us out.　追い出されるまでいよう。

Let's go to a café later.　*Ato-de kafe-e ikō.*
後でカフェへ行こう。

May I see you again?　*Mata aeru?*
また会える？

I'd like to try your home cooking.	***Anata-no teryōri-ga tabetai.*** ♀ あなたの手料理が食べたい。 ***Kimi-no teryōri-ga tabetai.*** ♂ 君の手料理が食べたい。
What's your best dish?	***Tokui-ryōri-wa nani?*** 得意料理は何？
I want to try that.	***Sore tabete-mitai.*** それ食べてみたい。
Can we meet tomorrow?	***Ashita aeru?*** 明日会える？
Can you go out this Saturday?	***Kondo-no doyōbi derareru?*** 今度の土曜日出られる？

This means "Can you get out of the house this Saturday?" Use...
dekakerareru? 出かけられる？ for "Can you go out with me...?"

I can't wait till then.	***Sore-made matenai.*** それまで待てない。
I can wait till then.	***Sore-made materu.*** それまで待てる。 ***Matsu-wa.*** ♀ 待つわ。 ***Matsu-yo.*** ♂ 待つよ。
I like holding your hand.	***Anata-to te-o tsunagu-noga suki.*** ♀ あなたと手をつなぐのが好き。 ***Kimi-to te-o tsunagu-noga suki.*** ♂ 君と手をつなぐのが好き。

Kiss me.	**Kisu shite.** キスして。

Kiss me deeply.	**Oishii kisu shite.** おいしいキスして。

This is another use of "**oishii**"—see chapter, Eating and Drinking. The Japanese almost always translate **oishii** as "delicious" —an appropriate image here!

I like kissing you.	**Anata-ni kisu-suru-noga suki.** ♀ あなたにキスするのが好き。 **Kimi-ni kisu-suru-noga suki.** ♂ 君にキスするのが好き。
You're a good kisser.	**Kisu-ga jōzu.** キスが上手。
Your lips are so soft.	**Anata-no kuchibiru-wa totemo ii-wa.** ♀ あなたの唇はとてもいいわ。 **Kimi-no kuchibiru-wa totemo ii-ne.** ♂ 君の唇はとてもいいね。
You're the only one I want.	**Atashi-ga hoshii-no-wa anata-dake.** ♀ あたしが欲しいのはあなただけ。 **Boku-ga hoshii-no-wa kimi-dake.** ♂ 僕が欲しいのは君だけ。

I can't wait to tell you.	*Sugoku hanashitai koto-ga aru-no.* ♀ すごく話したい事があるの。 *Sugoku hanashitai koto-ga arun-da-kedo.* すごく話したい事があるんだけど。

Use this to show your excitement/enthusiasm just before saying what's on your mind, inviting your friend to ask *Nani? Nani?* 荷？荷？ "What?"

I can't think of anything but you.	*Anata-no-koto igai-wa kangae-rarenai.* ♀ あなたの事以外は考えられない。 *Kimi-no-koto igai-wa kangae-rarenai.* ♂ 君の事以外は考えられない。
I can't live without you(r love).	*Anata-nashi-ja ikirarenai.* ♀ あなた無しじゃ生きられない。 *Kimi-nashi-ja ikirarenai.* ♂ 君無しじゃ生きられない。
It hurts to be without you.	*Anata-nashi-da to tsurai.* ♀ あなた無しだとつらい。 *Kimi-nashi-da to tsurai.* ♂ 君無しだとつらい。
Say you'll be mine.	*Atashi-no mono-to itte.* ♀ あたしのものと言って。 *Boku-no mono-to itte.* ♂ 僕のものと言って。
I'll make you happy.	*Shiawase-ni suru-yo.* ♂ 幸せにするよ。

Girls might take this as a proposal.

I've never felt this way
before.

Konna kimochi-ni natta-koto-nai.
こんな気持ちになったことない。

We had fun together,
didn't we?

Tanoshikatta-nē?
楽しかったねえ。
Tanoshikatta-nā? ♂
楽しかったなあ。

Do you remember our
first date?

Hajimete-no dēto oboeteru?
初めてのデート覚えてる？

Look into my eyes.

Atashi-no me-o mite. ♀
あたしの目を見て。
Boku-no me-o mite. ♂
僕の目を見て。

Stay just a little bit
longer.

Mō chotto-dake issho-ni-iyō.
もうちょっとだけ一緒にいよう。

I couldn't have done it
without you.

Anata-nishi-ja dekinakatta. ♀
あなた無しじゃできなかった。
Kimi-nashi-ja dekinakatta. ♂
君無しじゃできなかった。

Stay with me tonight.

*Konya-wa atashi-to issho-ni
ite.* ♀
今夜はあたしと一緒にいて。
*Konya-wa boku-to issho-ni
ite.* ♂
今夜は僕と一緒にいて。

I'll tell you something—
I love you.

Chotto kiite—(anata-ga) suki.
ちょっと聞いて、（あなたが）好き。
Chotto kiite—suki da-yo. ♂
ちょっと聞いて、好きだよ。

Saying "love" in Japanese can be a bit tricky. *Ai* (愛) is the direct translation of "love," but it's generally only for movie titles or as a joke. In normal conversation, you usually say *suki* (好き) and convey the feeling of love by the emotion and emphasis in your voice.

I know what's on your mind.

Anata-ga nani kangaeteru-ka shitteru. ♀
あなたが何考えてるか知ってる。

Kimi-ga nani kangaeteru-ka shitteru-yo. ♂
君が何考えてるか知ってるよ。

No, you don't.

Wakaruwakenai-deshō. ♀
分る訳ないでしょう。

Wakaruwakenai-darō. ♂
分る訳ないだろう。

You're thinking dirty thoughts.

Anata-wa yarashii-koto kangaeteru deshō. ♀
あなたはやらしいこと考えてるでしょう。

Kimi-wa yarashii-koto kangaeterun janai-no? ♂
君はやらしいこと考えてるんじゃないの？

So are you.

Anata-mo. ♀
あなたも。

Kimi-mo. ♂
君も。

I like that kind of thinking.

Sō-iu kangae suki.
そういう考え好き。

You're the only one I love.

Suki-na-no-wa anata-dake. ♀
好きなのはあなただけ。

Suki-na-no-wa kimi-dake. ♂
好きなのは君だけ。

Go easy (at first) on the sweet talk. Japanese boys don't throw around a lot of compliments or terms of endearment, so most girls are not accustomed to such attention. However, in the long run, most will definitely enjoy it.

I don't love anyone else.　　*Hoka-no dare-mo suki-janai.*
　　　　　　　　　　　　　　　他の誰も好きじゃない。

I love you so much I　　　　*Shinu-hodo suki.*
could die.　　　　　　　　　死ぬほど好き。

I love you for who you　　　*Sonomama-no anata-ga suki.* ♀
are.　　　　　　　　　　　　そのままのあなたが好き。
　　　　　　　　　　　　　　　Sonomama-no kimi-ga suki. ♂
　　　　　　　　　　　　　　　そのままの君が好き。

Now is the right time.　　　*Ima-ga sono-toki-yo.* ♀
　　　　　　　　　　　　　　　今がその時よ。
　　　　　　　　　　　　　　　Ima-ga sono-toki-dayo. ♂
　　　　　　　　　　　　　　　今がその時だよ。

Hold me tight.　　　　　　*Shikkari dakishimete.* ♀
　　　　　　　　　　　　　　　しっかり抱き締めて。
　　　　　　　　　　　　　　　Tsuyoku dakishimete. ♀
　　　　　　　　　　　　　　　強く抱き締めて。

See me tonight.　　　　　　*Konya atte.*
　　　　　　　　　　　　　　　今夜会って。

I don't want to go home　　 *Konya-wa uchi-ni kaeritaku-*
tonight.　　　　　　　　　　*nai.* ♀
　　　　　　　　　　　　　　　今夜は家に帰りたくない。

A popular phrase. If she says this, pat yourself on the back.

Do you want to come to　　 *Uchi-ni kuru?*
my place?　　　　　　　　　家に来る？

I don't want to be used.　　*Asobaretakunai.*
　　　　　　　　　　　　　　　遊ばれたくない。

Asobu 遊ぶ means "to play." This passive form literally means "to be played/mucked around with."

Believe in me. **(Trust me.)**	***Atashi-o shinjite.*** ♀ あたしを信じて。 ***Boku-o shinjite.*** ♂ 僕を信じて。

I want to know all about
   you.
	Anata-no-koto subete
	   shiritai. ♀
	あなたのこと全て知りたい。
	Kimi-no-koto subete shiritai. ♂
	君のこと全て知りたい。

You're so very precious.	***Anata-wa tottemo taisetsu-na***
	   hito-yo. ♀
	あなたはとっても大切な人よ。
	Kimi-wa tottemo taisetsu-na
	   hito-nan-da. ♂
	君はとっても大切な人なんだ。

This is a very powerful expression of love and devotion. Use with caution.

I want to make love
   to you.
	Beddo-in shiyō. ♂
	ベッドインしよう。
	(Kimi-to) beddo-in shitai/
	   shiyō(-ze). ♂
	(君と) ベッドイン したい／
	   しよう (ぜ)。

Beddo-in means "go to bed." Guys can add **ze** ぜ to the end of many phrases for more punch (though also more roughness, be careful). And this is sometimes used (among good friends) as a joke, so don't take it seriously every time!

Making Love 6

It's too early (to go to bed).

Mada hayai.
まだ早い。

Take me tonight.

Konya daite. ♀
今夜抱いて。

Literally means "Hold me."

Etchi shiyō.
エッチしよう。
Etchi suru?
エッチする？
Etchi shitainā. ♂
エッチしたいなあ。

Japanese do not often directly say "Let's go to bed." Instead the words are conveyed by the mood. These phrases are useful in case you miss the mood signals.

Shall we go to a love hotel?

Rabu hoteru-ni ikō-ka?
ラブホテルに行こうか。
Rabu ho-ni ikō-ka?
ラブホに行こうか。

Young Japanese usually live with their parents right up to their wedding day. With small houses or apartments and paper-thin walls, the living arrangements are not conducive to good sex. Owning a car provides little escape, for there are few pleasant, obscure places to park short of driving two or three hours to the countryside. So, where do the non-farmers go for a roll in the hay? Have you heard of a love hotel? No? Then step this way...

Identifying a love hotel is easy, as most of them are near big train stations (four tracks or more), in entertainment districts, and along major highways.

They are usually well-lit with colorful Japanese characters or **rōmaji** in neon, or just a sign saying "Hotel," with some twinkling stars floating around it. If there are no obvious markings, look for big, big objects on the roof. A 30-foot mock Statue of Liberty or Queen Elizabeth (the ship, that is) on top of a building that has no other visible ads or signs is a dead giveaway. Also, the absence of a doorman and a lobby with a front desk should scream love hotel.

The service at a love hotel is very discreet; you don't see them and they don't see you. ID's aren't even checked, as there's a rule of thumb: if you're old enough to pay, you're old enough to play.

Come closer to me.	***Motto soba-ni konai?*** (voiced softly) もっとそばに来ない？
I'm so glad I waited.	***Machi kutabireta.*** 待ちくたびれた。 ***Machi kutabireta-yo.*** ♂ 待ちくたびれたよ。

Your hair smells good.	***Anata-no kami(noke) ii kaori-ga*** ***suru.*** ♀ あなたの髪(の毛) いい香りがする。 ***Kimi-no kaminoke ii kaori-ga*** ***suru-ne.*** ♂ 君の髪(の毛) いい香りがするね。
What perfume/cologne are you wearing?	***Nanno kōsui/koron tsuketeru-*** ***no?*** 何の香水／コロンつけてるの？

What color underwear are you wearing (today)?

(Kyō) Nani iro-no shitagi tsuketeru-no?
(今日) 何色の下着つけてるの？

I like your underwear.

Sono shitagi kawaii-ne.
その下着かわいいね。

Sono shitagi kawaii-na. ♂
その下着かわいいな。

Kawaii literally means "cute."

That tickles.

Kusuguttai.
くすぐったい。

Kusuguttai-yo ♂
くすぐったいよ。

You have beautiful skin.

Hada kirei-dane. ♂
肌きれいだね。

I found your birthmark.

Kokoni hokuro-o mitsuketa.
ここにほくろを見つけた。

I'm getting excited.

Waku-waku-shitekichatta.
わくわくしてきちゃった。

Will you use a condom?

Gomu tsukete. ♀
ゴムつけて。

I'll use a condom.

Gomu tsukeru. ♂
ゴムつける。

Are you on the Pill?

Piru nonderu? ♂
ピル飲んでる？

Using the Pill is sometimes associated with depression, so guys may be better off assuming that she isn't on the Pill, and use a condom.

When was your first experience?	**Saisho-ni shita-no-wa itsu?** 最初にしたのはいつ？
Where was your first experience?	**Saisho doko-de shita?** 最初どこでした？
I did it at ...	**...-de shita-no.** ♀ ...でしたの。 **...-de shita.** ♂ ...でした。
I won't tell you.	**Oshiete agenai.** ♀ 教えてあげない。 **Oshienai.** 教えない。
Do you like to do it in the shower/bath?	**Shawā/Ofuro-de suru-no ga suki?** シャワー／お風呂でするのが 好き？
Do you like to do it in the morning?	**Asa suru-no-ga suki?** 朝するのが好き？
Do you masturbate?	**Musu/onanī suru?** マス／オナニーする？
Just joking.	**Uso/Jōdan-dayo.** 嘘／冗談だよ。
Buttocks	**oshiri** おしり **ketsu** ♂ けつ
Waist	**koshi** 腰

There is no word for "hips" in Japanese—**koshi** is as close as it gets.

Belly button	**oheso** おへそ

Breast(s)	***oppai***
	おっぱい
	mune
	胸
Nipple(s)	***chikubi***
	ちくび
Ear lobe	***mimitabu***
	耳たぶ
Nape of the neck	***unaji***
	うなじ

Japanese men find this especially erotic.

Down there	***asoko***
	あそこ

Asoko usually means "over there" but in this sense it means the "private parts."

Bush	***asoko-no ke*** ♂
	あそこの毛

As above, this means "the hair down there."

Cunt	***omanko*** ♂
	おまんこ
	omeko ♂
	おめこ

Omanko is used in the **Kantō** (greater Tōkyō) area, and **omeko** is preferred in the **Kansai** (greater Ōsaka).

Cock	***chinchin***
	ちんちん
Hard-on	***chinchin-ga tatsu*** ♂
	ちんちんが立つ
	bokki suru ♂
	ぼっきする
To come	***gamanjiru*** ♂
	我慢汁
	seishi
	精子

Gamanjiru is more like the preliminary shot before the ecstatic blast (*seishi*).

"swallowing"	*shabutte* ♂
	しゃぶって。
	sakku ♂
	サック
	fera ♂
	フェラ

Fera is more vulgar—if you're asking your girlfriend, it's better to say *sakku*.

balls	*kintama*
	金玉

Naturally enough, the words marked for guys only are pretty vulgar, and shouldn't be used when there are girls around! And Japanese girls tend to be very vague about these parts of the body, preferring to say *asoko* and to make allusions.

Lick my nipples.	*Chikubi o namete.* ♀
	ちくびをなめて。

Sixty-nine.	*Shikkusu-nain.*
	シックスナイン。

It's "six-nine" in Japanese, not "sixty-nine."

I like to "sixty-nine."	*Shikkusu-nain suki.*
	シックスナイン好き。

Let's do "sixty-nine."	*Shikkusu-nain-de shiyō.*
	シックスナインでしよう。

Show me what turns you on/stimulates you.	*Doko-ga kanjiru-ka oshiete.*
	どこが感じるか教えて。

I like to try different styles.	*Chigau tai'i-de suru-no ga suki.*
	違う体位でするのが好き。

Let's try a different style.	***Chigau tai'i-de shiyō.*** 違う体位でしよう。

Think of a new position.	***Atarashii tai'i-o kangaete.*** 新しい体位を考えて。
I'm tired of that one.	***Are-niwa akita.*** あれには飽きた。
That's original.	***Kore-wa orijinaru.*** これはオリジナル。
That sounds exciting.	***Dokidoki-shichau.*** どきどきしちゃう。 ***Dokidoki-suru.*** どきどきする。 ***Wakuwaku-shichau.*** わくわくしちゃう。 ***Wakuwaku-suru.*** わくわくする。

Wakuwaku-shichau/suru can also be used in nonsexual contexts such as "That party sounds exciting."

Let's do it again.	***Mō ikkai shiyō.*** もう1回しよう。
Missionary position/ Girl bottom/boy top	***Seijōi*** 正常位
Boy bottom/girl top	***Kijōi*** 騎乗位

Doggy style	***Bakku***
	バック
	Kōbai
	後背位

Seijōi literally means "normal"; *Kijōi* means "to ride"; and ***bakku*** means, well, you know. To express "Let's do it doggy style," one would say ***Bakku shiyō***; for "Let's use the missionary position," one would say ***Seijōi-de shiyō***.

I forgot to use a condom.	***Gomu wasurechatta.*** ♂
	ゴム忘れちゃった。
Did it hurt?	***Itakunakatta?*** ♂
	痛くなかった？
It did!	***Itakatta!*** ♀
	痛かった！
No, it didn't.	***Itakunakatta(no).*** ♀
	痛くなかった（の）。
Do Japanese couples have car sex?	***Nihon-no kappuru-wa kā-sekkusu suru-no?***
	日本のカップルはカーセックス するの？
Yes, but not often.	***Un, demo sonna-ni yaranai.***
	うん、でもそんなにやらない。
No. There aren't any good places.	***Uun, ii basho-ga nai.***
	ううん、いい場所がない。
Where do they go?	***Minna doko-ni iku-no?***
	みんなどこに行くの？
Let's find a good place.	***Ii basho-o sagasō.***
	いい場所を探そう。
How do you know of such a place?	***Sonna basho nande shitteru-no?***
	そんな場所何で知ってるの？
People can see us here.	***Koko-ja hito-ni miechau-yo.***
	ここじゃ人に見えちゃうよ。

That'll make it more exciting.

Shigeki-teki. ♀
刺激的。

Shigeki-teki-dane. ♂
刺激的だね。

Let's get in the back seat.

Bakku shiito-ni suwarō.
バックシートに座ろう。

Let's recline the front seats.

Furonto shiito-o taosō.
フロントシートを倒そう。

Let's use the blanket.

Mōfu-o tsukaō.
毛布を使おう。

The blanket's dirty.

Mōfu kitanai-nē.
毛布汚いねえ。

Take your shoes off.

Kutsu-o nugi-nayo. ♂
靴を脱ぎなよ。

Relax.

Rirakkusu-shite.
リラックスして。

Enjoy yourself.

Enjoi-shite.
エンジョイして。

Take your...off.

Shoes: *Kutsu-o nuide.*
靴を脱いで。

Bra: *Burajā-o hazushite.*
ブラジャーをはずして。

Underwear: *Shitagi-o totte.*
下着をとって。

Clothes: *Yōfuku-o nuide.*
洋服を脱いで。

I'm cold.	*Samui.* 寒い。
Make me warm.	*Atatamete.* 暖めて。 *Attamete.* あっためて。
Doesn't that feel better?	*Sono-hō-ga kimochi yokunai?* その方が気持ちよくない？
Do it like this.	*Konna-fū-ni shite.* こんなふうにして。
That's right.	*Sō-dane.* そうだね。 *Sō-dana.* ♂ そうだな。 *Māne.* まあね。

Māne is often used to mean "I know." If said teasingly, it means "Yeah, I know (but I might not tell you)."

I made love.	*Yacchatta.* やっちゃった。

This literally means "I did it"—you'll be clear by the context!

In Japanese there is a slang use of "A," "B," and "C" similar to the American English slang use of "first base," "second base," "third base," and "home run." These letters denote kissing, petting, and making love, respectively, so you could say *A shita* エーした etc.

I scored (with her).	*Nampa-shita.* ♂ なんぱした。

Nampa means "dishonest person" and the opposite, *kōha* こうは, means "honest person." A *nampa* might ask to make love on the first date, whereas a *kōha* might wait till their wedding night. In this context, *Nampa-shita* means "I went girl hunting (successfully)." This is a boy's phrase because only girls get nampa'd. (*Kōha-shita* doesn't mean anything.) A *nampa-yarō* is a boy who likes girl hunting.

Oops!

7

I have some good news. *Ii shirase-ga arun-da.* ♀
いい知らせがあるんだ。

I can't tell you on the phone. *Denwa-ja ienai.* ♀
電話じゃ言えない。

You're going to be a father! *Anata-wa papa-ni naru-noyo!* ♀
あなたはパパになるのよ！

I'm pregnant. *Atashi ninshin shiteru-no.* ♀
あたし妊娠してるの。

Congratulations! *Omedetō!* ♂
おめでとう！

Are you sure? *Hontō-ni?* ♂
本当に？

I haven't had my period yet. *Seiri-ga konai-no.* ♀
生理が来ないの。

When was your last period? *Saigo-no seiri-wa itsu kita-no?* ♂
最後の生理はいつ来たの？

Maybe it was too early to take the test. *Kensa-o suru-ni-wa hayasugirun-janai.* ♂
検査をするには早過ぎるん
じゃない。

Take the test again.	**Mō ikkai kensa shitemite.** ♂ もう1回検査してみて。
When did you find out?	**Itsu wakatta-no?** ♂ いつ分かったの？
Why didn't you tell me sooner?	**Nande motto hayaku iwanakatta-no?** ♂ 何でもっと早く言わなかったの？
I've been wanting to tell you, but (I didn't)...	**Iitakatta-kedo...** ♀ 言いたかったけど...。
What week are you now?	**Ima nan-shū-me?** ♂ 今何週目？
When's the baby due?	**Yoteibi-wa itsu?** ♂ 予定日はいつ？
It's going to change our lives.	**Korekara isogashiku naru-ne.** ♂ これから忙しくなるね。

Literally means "We're going to get busy from now on..."

I want a boy/girl.	**Otoko-no-ko/Onna-no-ko-ga ii.** 男の子／女の子がいい。
It is/was our destiny.	**Kitto unmei dattan-dane.** きっと運命だったんだね。
There's no better news than this.	**Kore-ijō ureshii koto wa nai-yo.** ♂ これ以上嬉しい事はないよ。
When will your stomach show?	**Itsu-goro-kara onaka-ga ōkiku naru-no?** ♂ いつごろからお腹が大きくなるの？
Take good care of yourself.	**Muri shinai yō-nine.** ♂ 無理しないようにね。

(We should) start reading books about babies.

Sorosoro akachan-no hon-o yomi-hajimetara? ♂

そろそろ赤ちゃんの本を読み始めたら？

We should think of a name.

Namae-o kangae-nakucha.

名前を考えなくちゃ。

Are you sure it's mine?

Hontō-ni boku-no-ko? ♂

本当に僕の子？

I won't answer that/ That's a crazy question!

Nande sonna-koto kiku-no? ♀

何でそんな事聞くの？

I guess that our protection wasn't good enough.

Chanto gomu tsukenakattan-dane. ♂

ちゃんとゴムつけなかったんだね。

You said it was safe.

Gomu tsuketeta-tte itta-jan. ♀

ゴムつけてたって言ったじゃん。

I can't be held responsible.

Boku-ni sekinin wa nai. ♂

僕に責任はない。

Take responsibility.

Sekinin-o totte. ♀

責任をとって。

Don't run away from your responsibility.

Chanto kangaete-yo. ♀

ちゃんと考えてよ。

This is a useful and very "Japanese" phrase—it literally means "think about it well," but it carries the nuance of "you have to do this."

You knew it could happen, didn't you?	**Kō-naru-kamo shirenai-tte wakattetan-janai-no?** こうなるかもしれないって分かってたんじゃないの？
See you later.	**Ato-de-ne.** ♀ 後でね。 **Ato-de-na.** ♂ 後でな。
Don't call me.	**Denwa-shinaide.** 電話しないで。
I'll call you later.	**Atashi-ga ato-de denwa-suru.** ♀ あたしが後で電話する。 **Boku-ga ato-de denwa-suru.** ♂ 僕が後で電話する。
You'll be sorry.	**Kōkai-suru-yo.** こうかいするよ。
It's a bad time.	**Taimingu-ga warui.** タイミングが悪い。
It's too early.	**Hayasugiru.** 早過ぎる。
It's your fault.	**Anata-no sei.** ♀ あなたのせい。 **Kimi-no sei.** ♂ 君のせい。
Please give it up this time/ let's stop arguing.	**Gomen-ne, akiramete.** ごめんね、諦めて。
We have to think about it carefully.	**Motto yoku kangaenakucha.** もっとよく考えなくちゃ。
I wish it were a dream.	**Yume-dattara yokatta-noni.** 夢だったらよかったのに。
What will happen to us?	**Atashitachi dō narun-darō?** ♀ あたしたちどうなるんだろう？

	Bokutachi dō narun-darō? ♂
	僕たちどうなるんだろう？
What do we do now?	**Dō-suru?**
	どうする？
I don't know what to do.	**Dō-shitara ii-ka wakannai.**
	どうしたらいいか分かんない。
Let's decide together.	**Futari-de kimeyō.**
	二人で決めよう。
	Issho-ni kimeyō.
	一緒に決めよう。
	Issho-ni kangaeyō.
	一緒に考えよう。
It's up to you.	**Anata-ni makaseru.** ♀
	あなたに任せる。
	Kimi-ni makaseru. ♂
	君に任せる。
You decide.	**Anata-ga kimete.** ♀
	あなたが決めて。
	Kimi-ga kimete. ♂
	君が決めて。
Let me think it over.	**Mō ichido kangae-sasete.**
	もう1度考えさせて。
Whatever you want to do will be fine with me.	**Anata-ga shitai-yō-ni shite-ii-wa.** ♀
	あなたがしたいようにしていいわ。
	Kimi-ga shitai-yō-ni shite-ii-yo. ♂
	君がしたいようにしていいよ。
The child is ours, not just mine.	**Akachan-wa atashi-dake-no mono-janai-wa.** ♀
	赤ちゃんはあたしだけのものじゃ ないわ。

I don't have enough money.

Sonna-ni okane nai-yo.
そんなにお金ないよ。

I'll earn the money (for it).

Okane-o yōi suru-wa. ♀
お金を用意するわ。

Okane-o yōi suru-yo. ♂
お金を用意するよ。

I can get it.

Atsumerareru-yo.
集められるよ。

Will you go with me?

Atashi-to issho-ni kite-kureru? ♀
あたしと一緒に来てくれる？

Do you have to stay in the hospital (overnight)?

Nyūin shinakucha ikenai-no?
入院しなくちゃいけないの？

Is there anything I can do for you?

Nanika atashi-ni dekiru-koto aru? ♀
何かあたしにできる事ある？

Nanika boku-ni dekiru-koto aru? ♂
何か僕にできる事ある？

I just can't do it.

Konna-koto dekinai.
こんな事できない。

Love and Marriage

When do you want to get married?	*Itsu-goro kekkon-shitai?* いつごろ結婚したい？
At what age do you want to marry?	*Nansai-de kekkon-shitai?* 何歳で結婚したい？
Are you going to work after you're married?	*Kekkon-shitemo hatarakitai?* 結婚しても働きたい？
Do you think you're ready to get married?	*Kekkon-suru kokoro-no junbi-wa dekiteru?* 結婚する心の準備はできてる？

These four are "beating around the bush" questions to check if it's OK to ask the big question.

Why all these questions about marriage?	*Nande kekkon-no-koto bakkari iu no?* 何で結婚の事ばっかり言うの？

Stop beating around the bush!	*Gocha-gocha iwanaide!* ごちゃごちゃ言わないで！
Are you trying to propose to me?	*Puropōzu-shiyō-to shiteru-no?* プロポーズしようとしてるの？

What's the question? *Nani-ga iitai-no?*
何が言いたいの？

What's the answer? *Kotae-wa?*
答えは？

What's on your mind? *Nani kangaeteru-no?*
何 考えてるの？

Will you marry me? *Kekkon-shite-kureru?*
結婚してくれる？

If you don't want to say this, the following four phrases are substitutes, ranked subtle to direct.

Will you make miso soup for me? *Boku-no tame-ni misoshiru-o tsukutte-kureru?* ♂
僕のためにみそ汁を作ってくれる？

Miso soup is made with soybean paste. It can be eaten at any meal, but is an important item in a traditional Japanese breakfast...

Will you use my last name? *Boku-no myōji-ni natte-kureru?* ♂
僕の名字になってくれる？

Shall we share the rest of our lives together? *Kore kara-mo zutto issho-ni ite-kurenai?*
これからもずっと一緒にいてくれない？

Will you have my baby? *Boku-no kodomo-o unde-kurenai?* ♂
僕の子供を産んでくれない？

I can't marry you. *Anata-towa kekkon-dekinai.* ♀
あなたとは結婚できない。
Kimi-towa kekkon-dekinai. ♂
君とは結婚できない。

I don't want to marry you. *Anata-towa kekkon-shitaku-nai.* ♀
あなたとは結婚したくない。
Kimi-towa kekkon-shitaku-nai. ♂
君とは結婚したくない。

I can't get married now.

Ima-wa kekkon-dekinai.
今は結婚できない。

Why not?

Nande-nano?
何でなの？

Nande (dame-nano)?
何で(だめなの)？

Let's get married.

Kekkon shiyō.
結婚しよう。

What are you going to do about your job/ school?

Shigoto/Gakkō-o dō-suru tsumori?
仕事／学校をどうするつもり？

Are you going to quit work/school?

Shigoto/Gakkō-o yameru tsumori?
仕事／学校を辞めるつもり？

I should get a better paying job.

Motto kyūryō-no ii shigoto-o sagasanakucha.
もっと給料のいい仕事を探さなくちゃ。

I'd better get a second job.

Arubaito-o shita-hō-ga ii-ne.
アルバイトをした方がいいね。

Arubaito-o shita-hō-ga ii-na. ♂
アルバイトをした方がいいな。

This literally means "I'd better do some part-time work," and if you're not working, this is what it means—but if you're already doing one job, it means you're thinking of getting another one.

I don't want my wife to work.

Boku-no okusan-ni-wa hataraite hoshikunai. ♂
僕の奥さんには働いて欲しくない。

I'm sure the neighbors will talk about us.

Kinjo-no-hitotachi atashitachi-no-koto hanasu-deshō-ne. ♀
近所の人たちあたしたちの事話す
でしょうね。

Kinjo-no-hitotachi bokutachi-no-koto hanasu-darō-ne. ♂
近所の人たち僕たちのこと話す
だろうね。

Are you worried about what your neighbors might say?

Kinjo-no-hito-ga nante iu-ka ki-ni naru?
近所の人が何て言うか気になる？

Does your family care what the neighbors say?

Kinjo-no-hito-ga iu-koto anata-no kazoku ki-ni suru? ♀
近所の人が言う事あなたの家族
気にする？

Kinjo-no-hito-ga iu-koto kimi-no kazoku ki-ni suru? ♂
近所の人が言う事君の家族
気にする？

Are you going to support your parents in their old age?

Ryōshin-no rōgo-no mendō miru-no?
両親の老後の面倒見るの？

I should tell my parents.

Oya-ni itta-hō ga ii.
親に言った方がいい。

I should call my parents.	*Oya-ni denwa-shinakucha.* 親に電話しなくちゃ。
What will your parents think?	*Anata-no oya-wa dō omou- kanā?* ♀ あなたの親はどう思うかなあ？
	Kimi-no oya-wa dō omou- darō? ♂ 君の親はどう思うだろう？
I have already told my parents.	*Mō oya-ni itta.* もう親に言った。
What did they say?	*Nante itteta?* 何て言ってた？
Were they mad?	*Okotteta?* 怒ってた？
Are your parents on our side?	*Anata-no oya atashitachi-no koto wakatte-kureta?* ♀ あなたの親あたしたちの事 分かってくれた？
	Kimi-no oya bokutachi-no koto wakatte-kureta? ♂ 君の親僕たちの事分かって くれた？
Will your parents help us?	*Anata-no oya tasukete-kureru- kanā?* ♀ あなたの親助けてくれるかなあ？
	Kimi-no oya tasukete-kureru- kanā? ♂ 君の親助けてくれるかなあ？
We can live with my parents for a while.	*Atashi-no oya-to shibaraku issho-ni sumeru-wa.* ♀ あたしの親としばらく一緒に 住めるわ。
	Boku-no oya-to shibaraku issho-ni sumeru-yo. ♂ 僕の親としばらく一緒に住めるよ。

How long is "a while?"	*'Shibaraku'-tte dono gurai?* 「しばらく」ってどのぐらい？
I should talk to your parents (about it).	*Anata-no oya-ni hanasa-nakucha.* ♀ あなたの親に話さなくちゃ。 *Kimi-no oya-ni hanasa-nakucha.* ♂ 君の親に話さなくちゃ。
Let me meet your parents.	*Anata-no oya-ni awasete.* ♀ あなたの親に会わせて。 *Kimi-no oya-ni awasete.* ♂ 君の親に会わせて。
Introduce me to your family.	*Anata-no kazoku-ni shōkai-shite.* ♀ あなたの家族に紹介して。 *Kimi-no kazoku-ni shōkai-shite.* ♂ 君の家族に紹介して。
When should I meet your parents?	*Itsu anata-no oya-ni attara ii-deshō?* ♀ いつあなたの親に会ったらいいでしょう？ *Itsu kimi-no oya-ni attara ii-darō?* ♂ いつ君の親に会ったらいいだろう？
I'll meet your parents as soon as possible.	*Dekiru-dake hayaku anata-no oya-ni au.* ♀ できるだけ早くあなたの親に会う。 *Dekiru-dake hayaku kimi-no oya-ni au.* ♂ できるだけ早く君の親に会う。
Now is as good a time as any.	*Itsu-demo onaji.* ♀ いつでも同じ。 *Itsu-demo onaji-dayo.* ♂ いつでも同じだよ。

Now is not a good time.	*Ima-wa yokunai.* 今はよくない。
Maybe I shouldn't meet your parents now.	*Tabun ima oya-ni awanai-hō-ga ii.* 多分今親に会わない方がいい。
May be some other time.	*Tabun chigau-hi.* 多分違う日。
We can do it later.	*Ato-de dekiru.* 後でできる。
Do you think your parents will accept our baby/ marriage?	*Anata-no oya atashitachi-no akachan/kekkon-o mitomete-kureru-kanā?* ♀ あなたの親あたしたちの赤ちゃん／結婚を認めてくれるかなあ？ *Kimi-no oya bokutachi-no akachan/kekkon-o mitomete-kureru-kanā?* ♂ 君の親僕たちの赤ちゃん／結婚を認めてくれるかなあ？

The acceptance of cross-cultural marriages (*kokusai kekkon* 国際結婚) is growing amongst progressive-thinking Japanese. But there are still hardened attitudes against them out there, and some parents are more "protective" of their eldest son or daughter, whom they expect to be there for them when they get old. They might be scared that a foreigner would whisk their eldest away!

Tell me what to do in front of your family.	*Anata-no kazoku-ni atta-toki dō-shitara ii-ka oshiete.* ♀ あなたの家族に会った時どうしたらいいか教えて。 *Kimi-no kazoku-ni atta-toki dō-shitara ii-ka oshiete.* ♂ 君の家族に会った時どうしたらいいか教えて。

You probably shouldn't kiss or hug in front of a girl's family until they know you really well. It's OK to hold hands though.

What should I talk about?	***Nani-o hanaseba ii?*** 何を話せばいい？
What shall I/we bring?	***Nani-o motte-ikō-ka?*** 何を持って行こうか。
Tell me what to say.	***Nante ittara ii-ka oshiete.*** 何て言ったらいいか教えて。
Do you think your family will like me?	***Anata-no kazoku atashi-no-koto ki-ni-itte-kureru-kanā?*** ♀ あなたの家族あたしの事気に入ってくれるかなあ？ ***Kimi-no kazoku boku-no-koto ki-ni-itte-kureru-kanā?*** ♂ 君の家族僕の事気に入ってくれるかなあ？
Does your father smoke?	***Otōsan tabako suu?*** お父さんタバコ吸う？
Does your father drink?	***Otōsan osake nomu?*** お父さんお酒飲む？
What's your father's hobby/work?	Otōsan-no shumi/shigoto-wa nani? お父さんの趣味／仕事は何？

Typical jobs are ***kaishain*** 会社員, company worker; ***sarariiman*** サラリーマン, office worker; ginkōin 銀行員, banker. The answer will probably be something like one of the first two (vague) replies. After that, it's (usually!) OK to ask what company he works for *Dokono kaisha de hataraite-maska?* どこの会社で働いてますか? (to his face), but don't push regarding his position.

What's your mother's hobby/work?	*Okāsan-no shumi/shigoto-wa nani?* お母さんの趣味／仕事は何?

Japan is still a very sexist society, and women's work is usually lower-ranking than men's. Typical jobs include OL, office lady; *shufu* 主婦, housewife and *arubaito* アルバイト part-time work. If the answer is *atashi OL desu* (I'm an OL—office lady), it's probably OK to ask what company she works for *Doko no kaisha de hataraite-maska?* どこの会社で働いてますか? (to her face), but certainly don't ask for more information if she says *arubaito shitemas* アルバイトしてます。(I work part-time)— she may be embarrassed and prefer not to say.

Who might oppose our marriage?	*Dare-ka atashitachi-no kekkon hantai-suru-kanā?* ♀ 誰かあたしたちの結婚を反対するかなあ?
	Dare-ka bokutachi-no kekkon hantai-suru-kanā? ♂ 誰か僕たちの結婚を反対するかなあ?
Who will support our marriage?	*Dare-ka atashitachi-no kekkon-o ōen-shite-kureru-kanā?* ♀ 誰かあたしたちの結婚を応援してくれるかなあ?
	Dare-ka bokutachi-no kekkon-o ōen-shite-kureru-kanā? ♂ 誰か僕たちの結婚を応援してくれるかなあ?

When you're meeting your other half's parents for the first time, politeness is the key—the first impression is vital! Here are some ideas for things to say...

How should I address you?	***Nante oyobi-shitara ii-deshō-ka?*** 何てお呼びしたらいいでしょうか？

This is no laughing matter—in Japan, children generally call their parents and in-laws *otōsan* and *okāsan*—but preferences vary. Getting this wrong is a very quick way to put noses out of joint! If they prefer *otōsan* and *okāsan*, you can then use third-person polite phrases like *Okāsan-no shumi-wa nan desu-ka*? to their faces.

Where are you from?	***(Otōsan/Okāsan-wa) Dochira-no goshusshin des-ka?*** （お父さん／お母さんは）どちらの ご出身ですか。

This is a more formal and suitable question than *Dokkara kita-no*?, and unless they know you know a lot about Japan, the answer will probably not be too specific, e.g. *Kyōto no shusshin des*. 京都の出身です (I'm from Kyōto).

Aaah yes, I've been there.	***Aa, sō des-ka. Watashi, itta-koto-ga arimasu.*** ♀ ああ、そうですか。わたし、 行ったことがあります。 ***Aa, sō des-ka. Boku, itta-koto-ga arimas.*** ♂ ああ、そうですか。僕、行ったこ とがあります。
Have you ever been to...?	***...-he itta-koto-ga arimas-ka?*** ...へ行ったことがありますか？
It's a very interesting/busy/ pretty/green city/ country, isn't it?	***Totemo omoshiroi/nigiyaka/kirei/ shizen-ga aru machi/tokoro des-ne.*** とても面白い／にぎやかな／ きれいな／自然がある 街／ところですね。
I played tennis while I was at school/ university.	***Kōkō/Daigaku-no koro tenisu-o yarimashita.*** 高校／大学の頃テニスをやり ました。

I was in the local tennis club.	*Komyunitī-no tenisu kurabu-ni haitte-imashita.* コミュニティーのテニスクラブに入っていました。
How much will the wedding cost?	*Kekkon-shiki-no hiyō ikura gurai kakaru-no?* 結婚式の費用いくらぐらいかかるの？
We have to hurry to have the wedding.	*Isoide kekkon-shiki-o agenakucha.* 急いで結婚式をあげなくちゃ。
We should begin preparing now.	*Ima-kara yōi-shita-hō-ga ii.* 今から用意した方がいい。
Should we have a Japanese or a Western-style wedding?	*Seiyō-shiki-to Nihon-shiki, docchi-ni suru?* 西洋式と日本式、どっちにする？
What's the difference?	*Nani-ga chigau-no?* 何が違うの？

Until recently, Japanese weddings followed a clear pattern. A Japanese-style wedding is performed by a **Shintō** しんとう priest, the bride and groom usually wear **kimono** 着物 and the guests are limited to family members. These days western-styled weddings are preferred.

Health

9

You have a nice figure.	*Sutairu ii-ne.* ♀
	スタイルいいね。
	Sutairu ii-na. ♂
	スタイルいいな。
You're slim.	*Yaseteru-ne.*
	やせてるね。
	Yaseteru-na. ♂
	やせてるな。
	Surimu-dane.
	スリムだね。
	Surimu-dana. ♂
	スリムだな。
Did you lose weight?	*Yaseta?*
	やせた？
Did you gain weight?	*Chotto futotta kanā?*
	ちょっと太ったかなあ？
	Futtota?
	太った？

As in the West, if you're going to ask this (to a girl especially), it's better to couch it softly!

Do you think I need to diet?	*Daietto-shita-hō-ga ii-to omou?*
	ダイエットした方がいいと思う？
No, I like the way you are now.	*Uun, sono-mama-de ii-yo.*
	うん、そのままでいいよ。
Maybe you could try dieting.	*Chotto daietto-shitara ii kanā.*
	ちょっとダイエットしたらいいかなあ。
You need to go on a diet.	*Daietto-shita-hō-ga ii-yo.*
	ダイエットした方がいいよ。

I'm on a diet now.	*Ima daietto-shiteru.* 今ダイエットしてる。
I'm a vegetarian.	*Atashi bejitarian.* ♀ あたしベジタリアン。 *Boku bejitarian.* ♂ 僕ベジタリアン。
I don't eat fried food.	*Agemono-wa tabenai.* 揚げ物は食べない。
I try not to eat sweet food (as much as I can).	*(Dekiru-dake) okashi-o tabenai-yō-ni suru/shiteru.* （できるだけ）お菓子を食べない ようにする／してる。
I can't live without McDonalds.	*Makudonarudo (Makku) nashi-ja ikirarenai.* マクドナルド（マック）無しじゃ 生きられない。
I don't have time to cook proper meals.	*Chanto shita ryōri-o tsukuru jikan-ga nai.* ちゃんとした料理を作る時間が ない。
We could try cooking together.	*Issho-ni ryōri shite mireba?* 一緒に料理してみれば？
I know some healthy restaurants.	*Herushī-na resutoran-o shitteru.* ヘルシーなレストランを知ってる。
You should eat less snacks.	*Oyatsu-o tabenai-hō-ga ii-ne.* おやつを食べない方がいいね。
You shouldn't drink so much beer.	*Bīru-o sonna-ni nomanai-hō-ga ii-ne.* ビールをそんなに飲まない方が いいね。
You should stop smoking.	*Tabako yameta-hō-ga ii-ne.* タバコ止めた方がいいね。

Stop smoking. *Tabako yamete.*
タバコ止めて。

Tabako yame-nayo.
タバコ止めなよ。

Smoking is bad for your health. *Tabako-wa karada-ni yokunai.*
タバコは体によくない。

You need to exercise. *Undō shita-hōga ii-yo.*
運動した方がいいよ。

Do you exercise? *Undō suru?*
運動する？

Do you like to exercise? *Undōsuki?*
運動好き？

Karada-o ugokasu-no ga suki?
体を動かすのが好き？

We can do it together. *Issho-ni shiyō-yo.*
一緒にしようよ。

What type of exercise do you do? *Donna undō suru-no?*
どんな運動するの？

I run three kilometers every day. *Mainichi san-kiro hashiru.*
毎日3キロ走る。

I go to the gym. *Jimu-ni iku.*
ジムに行く。

I go to the pool. *Pūru-ni iku.*
プールに行く。

I like to swim.   *Oyogu-no-ga suki.*

泳ぐのが好き。

After a good exercise session, say *Koshi-ga itai* 腰が痛い, which means "My back hurts." People listening to you will really think you had sex the night before and that is the reason for your back-ache.

I play soccer/tennis/golf.   Sakkā/tenisu/gorufu-o yaru.

サッカー／テニス／ゴルフをやる。

Curses and Insults

10

What a coincidence (seeing you here).	***Konna tokoro-de au-towa-ne*** こんな所で会うとはね。
Fancy seeing you in a place like this.	***Konna tokoro-de au-nante.*** こんな所で会うなんて。

These can be used with the same sarcastic intent as in English.

This is a pain (bother).	***Mendōkusai.*** 面倒臭い。

This common phrase is usually shortened to ***mendokusai*** めんどくさい。

Who does she/he think she/he is?	***Erasō-ni nani itten-no.*** ♀ 偉そうに何言ってんの。
	Erasō-ni nani itteru. ♂ 偉そうに何言ってる。
Public restroom.	***Kōshū benjo.*** 公衆便所

This implies that she'll let anyone "use" her.

She'll be used and then thrown away.	***Tabun yararete suterareru.*** ♂ 多分やられて捨てられる。

To say this to a girl, add **-yo** よ to the end of ***suterareru***. To say it to yourself, add **-noni** ーのに.

She's stupid!	***Aitsu baka-dayo!*** ♂ あいつばかだよ！

Baka is one word that varies hugely in strength between regions. In Kantō, it's a moderate insult; in Kansai, it's about as harsh as it gets—there, ***aho*** あほ has a similar strength to ***baka*** in Kantō.

Who farted?	***Dare-ga onara-shita?*** 誰がおならした？

You did.

Anata/(name)-ga shitan deshō. ♀
あなたがしたんでしょう。

Kimi/(name)-ga shitan darō. ♂
君がしたんだろう。

It was you/You're the one!

Jibun-deshō! ♀
自分でしょう！

Jibun-darō! ♂
自分だろう！

Best used when pointing someone out. It implies "on the contrary," after you've been accused of something.

Wrong!

Chigau-yo!
違うよ！

That's not right!

Chigau-mon! ♀
違うもん！

Chigau-wayo! ♀
違うわよ！

Chigau-yo!
違うよ！

Shut up!

Damatte-yo! ♀
黙ってよ！

Damare-yo! ♂
黙れよ！

Who do you think you are?

Erasō-ni iuna-yo! ♂
偉そうに言うなよ！

You're dirty!
(Your relationship is shameful.)

Kitanai!
汚い！

Don't be jealous!　　　　*Yakimochi yakuna-yo!* ♂
やきもちやくなよ！

This is a good response to any of the above phrases.

Grow up!　　　　*Kodomo janain-dakara.*
子供じゃないんだから。

This literally means "Because you're not a child."

Don't act like a child.　　*Kodomo-mitai-na mane
　　　　　　　　　　　　　　shinaide.* ♀
子供みたいなまねしないで。
*Kodomo-mitai-na mane
　　　　　　suruna.* ♂
子供みたいなまねするな。

Act your age.　　　　*Anata wa nansai/ikutsu?!* ♀
あなたは何歳／いくつ！？
Kimi wa nansai/ikutsu?! ♂
君は何歳／いくつ！？

This literally means "How old are you?"

Don't get too big for　　*Jū-nen hayai.*
　your boots.　　　　10年早い。

This literally means "Ten years early."

Don't make me laugh.　　*Warawasenaide.* ♀
笑わせないで。
Warawaeruna-yo. ♂
笑わせるなよ。

Stop acting stupid!/
Don't joke around
with me!

Fuzakenai-deyo! ♀
ふざけないでよ！
Fuzakeruna-yo! ♂
ふざけるなよ！
Fuzaken-ja nēyo! ♂
ふざけんじゃねえよ！ *

*This is used especially when someone is being cheeky or has underestimated the speaker's power or status.

You're crazy!

Ikareten-janai-no?
いかれてんじゃないの？
Kichigai!
気違い！

That's stupid!

Baka-mitai!
ばかみたい！
Baka-jan!
ばかじゃん！

-jan is a colloquial suffix which means the same as *-deshō?/-darō?* でしょう？／だろう？ or *-yonē?* よねえ？, i.e. asking the other person to confirm your opinion. Only people under the age of about 35 use *-jan*.

What you did was stupid! *Baka-da!*
ばかだ！

You're stupid!/
You're an idiot!

Baka!
ばか！
Baka-yarō! ♂
ばかやろう！

Don't act stupid!/
Stop acting stupid!

Baka yamete-yo! ♀
ばか止めてよ！
Baka yamero-yo! ♂
ばか止めろよ！
Baka yamena-yo! ♀
ばか止めなよ！
Baka yatten-ja nēyo! ♂
ばかやってんじゃねえよ！

What are you doing?	***Nani shiten-no?*** 何してんの？
What the hell are you doing?	***Nani yatten-no?*** 何やってんの？
You shouldn't have done that.	***Sore shinakya yokatta-noni.*** それしなきゃよかったのに。
How dare you!	***Nande sonna-koto dekiru-no!*** ♀ 何でそんな事できるの？ ***Nande sonna-koto dekirun-da!*** ♂ 何でそんな事できるんだ？
Don't you have something to do? (Stop bothering me!)	***Hoka-ni suru-koto-nai-no?*** 他にする事ないの？
You ain't got the balls!	***Konjō nashi!*** 根性なし！

Means you're lacking in courage.

	Chinchin chiisai! ♂ ちんちん小さい！

This literally means "You have a small penis!" As you'd expect, it's a very serious insult!

I've got guts!	***Konjō-wa arusa!*** 根性はあるさ！
Don't make me mad.	***Okorasenaide(yo).*** ♀ 怒らせないで(よ)。 Okoraseruna. ♂ 怒らせるな。
I'm going mad/Fuck this! (broad meaning).	***Mukatsuita.*** むかついた！ ***Mukatsuku.*** むかつく！

Fuck you!/Go to hell!

Kutabare! ♂
くたばれ！
Shine! ♂
死ね！

Get out of here!/Fuck off!

Kiero! ♂
きえろ！
Mukō itte-yo! ♀
向こうに行ってよ！
Acchi itte-yo! ♀
あっち行ってよ！
Acchi ike-yo! ♂
あっち行けよ！
Dokka icchimae-yo! ♂
どっか行っちまえよ！

I'm leaving!

Mō iku!
もう行く！
Mō iku-yo! ♂
もう行くよ！

It wasn't your day, was it?

Kyō-wa tsuite-nakatta-nē?
今日はついてなかったねえ。

It's boring, isn't it?

Tsumannai-nē?
つまんないねえ。

Do you feel comfortable in public with me?

Atashi-to issho-ni dearuku-no ki-ninaru? ♀
あたしと一緒に出歩くの気になる？

Boku-to issho-ni dearuku-no ki-ni naru? ♂
僕と一緒に出歩くの気になる？

I don't want you to get hurt on my account.

Atashi-no sei-de iya-na omoi sasetakunai. ♀
あたしのせいでいやな思いさせたくない。

Boku-no sei-de iya-na omoi sasetakunai. ♂
僕のせいでいやな思いさせたくない。

Do you care what they think?

Minna-ga dō omou-ka ki-ni naru?
皆がどう思うか気になる？

Don't let it bother you (what others think).

Hoka-no-hito-no-koto ki-ni shinaide. ♀
他の人のこと気にしないで。

Hoka-no-hito-no-koto ki-ni suruna-yo. ♂
他の人のこと気にするなよ。

Don't be upset.

Okoranaideyo. ♀
怒らないでよ。

Okoruna-yo. ♂
怒るなよ。

Does your family know about us?

Anata-no kazoku atashitachi-no-koto shitteru? ♀

あなたの家族あたしたちのこと
知ってる？

Kimi-no kazoku bokutachi-no-koto shitteru? ♂

君の家族僕たちのこと知ってる？

I told my family about you.

Kazoku-ni anata-no-koto hanashita. ♀

家族にあなたのこと話した。

Kazoku-ni kimi-no-koto hanashita. ♂

家族に君のこと話した。

Do you think we should see each other again?

Atashitachi mata attara ii-to omou? ♀

あたしたちまた会ったらいいと
思う？

Bokutachi mata attara ii-to omou? ♂

僕たちまた会ったらいいと思う？

Tell me, what do you think?

Dō omou? Oshiete.

どう思う？教えて。

Make it clear.

Hakkiri-shite.

はっきりして。

Please don't go.

Ikanaide.

行かないで。

You don't know.

Anata-wa shiranai to omou. ♀

あなたは知らないと思う。

Kimi-wa shiranai to omou. ♂

君は知らないと思う。

We've known each other for three months now.

Atashitachi shiriatte-kara sankagetsu-ni naru-no(ne). ♀

あたしたち知り合ってから3か月
になるの(ね)。

Bokutachi shiriatte-kara sanka-
getsu-ni naru-nā/ne. ♂
僕たち知り合ってから3か月に
なるなあ／ね。

When saying this to someone else, say... *ni naru-nā*. To your
partner, a final ne with a (slight) rising intonation is better.

We can make it work.   *Dō ni-ka naru-yo.*
どうにかなるよ。

I want to know what   *Anata-ga dō omotteru-ka*
you're feeling.   *shiritai.* ♀
あなたがどう思ってるか知りたい。

Kimi-ga dō omotteru-ka
shiritai. ♂
君がどう思ってるか知りたい。

It'll all change.   *Subete kawaru-yo.*
全て変わるよ。

Let's not get serious now. *Ima maji-ni naru-no-wa*
yameyō.
今まじになるのは止めよう。

The use of "let's" here is very Japanese, as it invites the other
party into the decision-making process, a part of the typical
Japanese subtlety. Directly stating one's wishes will halve the normal runaround, but will put off those who prefer indirectness.

I don't want to get serious. *Maji-ni naritakunai.*
まじになりたくない。

I don't (even) want to think about it.

Kangae-taku(-mo) nai.
考えたく(も)ない。

This is a very strong phrase—use it with care!

What does that mean?

Dō-iu imi?
どういう意味？

Don't cry/Wipe your tears away.

Nakanaide.
泣かないで。

Namida-o fuite.
涙を拭いて。

Don't be sad.

Kanashimanaide.
悲しまないで。

Cheer up.

Genki dashite.
元気出して。

Don't worry; be happy.

Shinpai-shinaide, genki dashite.
心配しないで、元気出して。

Let's talk about this later.

Sono-koto-wa ato-de hanasō.
その事は後で話そう。

Let's change the subject.

Chotto hanashi-ga kawaru kedo...
ちょっと話が変わるけど...。

Hanashi-o kaeyō.
話を変えよう。

By the way,...

Tokoro-de,...
ところで...

Don't change the subject.	*Hanashi-o kaenaide.* ♀ 話を変えないで。 *Hanashi-o kaeruna.* ♂ 話を変えるな。
Please listen to me/ Let me explain.	*(Tanomu kara) hanashi-o kiite.* (頼むから)話を聞いて。

Adding *Tanomu kara* makes this softer, much better if you're pleading, say after being knocked back.

I was only joking.	*Tada-no jōdan-dayo.* ただの冗談だよ。
Don't take it so seriously.	*Sonna-ni maji-ni toranaide.* ♀ そんなにまじに取らないで。 *Sonna-ni maji-ni toruna-yo.* ♂ そんなにまじに取るなよ。
I don't play around.	*Atashi-wa asondenai-wayo.* ♀ あたしは遊んでないわよ。 *Boku-wa asondenai-yo.* ♂ 僕は遊んでないよ。
I was busy playing around.	*Asobimakutteta.* 遊びまくってた。
Don't do that again.	*Mō sonna-koto shinaide.* もうそんな事しないで。
I'll forget about it.	*Mō sono-koto-wa ii-wa.* ♀ もうその事はいいわ。 *Mō sono-koto-wa ii-yo.* ♂ もうその事はいいよ。
I'm not mad anymore.	*Mō okottenai-wa.* ♀ もう怒ってないわ。 *Mō okottenai-yo.* ♂ もう怒ってないよ。

Are you still mad?　　　*Mada okotteru?*
　　　　　　　　　　　　　　まだ怒ってる？

You're still mad, aren't　　*Mada okotteru-deshō?* ♀
you?　　　　　　　　　　まだ怒ってるでしょう？
　　　　　　　　　　　　　　Mada okotteru-darō? ♂
　　　　　　　　　　　　　　まだ怒ってるだろう？

I think I was wrong.　　　*Atashi-ga machigatteta-wa.* ♀
　　　　　　　　　　　　　　あたしが間違ってたわ。
　　　　　　　　　　　　　　Boku-ga machigatteta-yo. ♂
　　　　　　　　　　　　　　僕が間違ってたよ。

I shouldn't have done　　*Shinakya yokatta.*
that.　　　　　　　　　　しなきゃよかった。
　　　　　　　　　　　　　　Surun-ja nakatta.
　　　　　　　　　　　　　　するんじゃなかった。

I don't know why I did　　*Nan-de sō shita-ka wakannai.*
that.　　　　　　　　　　何でそうしたか分かんない。

I think I was too excited.　*Sugoku moriagatteta.*
　　　　　　　　　　　　　　すごく盛り上がってた。
　　　　　　　　　　　　　　Sugoku wakuwaku shiteta.
　　　　　　　　　　　　　　すごくわくわくしてた。

I think I was too nervous.　*Chotto kinchō shiteta.*
　　　　　　　　　　　　　　ちょっと緊張してた。
　　　　　　　　　　　　　　Chotto ochikondeta.
　　　　　　　　　　　　　　ちょっと落ち込んでた。

I was out of my mind.　　*Jibun-demo naze-ka wakannai.*
　　　　　　　　　　　　　　自分でもなぜか分かんない。

It was silly of me (to do that).
Baka-na koto shita-nā.
ばかな事したなあ。

You have so much more than they do.
Anata-wa minna-ni nai mono-o motteru. ♀
あなたは皆にないものを持ってる。
Kimi-wa minna-ni nai mono-o motteru. ♂
君は皆にないものを持ってる。

If you change your mind, let me know.
Moshi ki-ga kawattara oshiete.
もし気が変わったら教えて。

What changed your mind?
Nan-de ki-ga kawatta-no?
何で気が変わったの？

I didn't mean to hurt you.
Kizutsukeru tsumori-wa nakatta.
傷付けるつもりはなかった。

I should've thought about it more.
Motto kangaereba yokatta.
もっと考えればよかった。

I hurt your feelings, didn't I?
Kanji warukatta deshō? ♀
感じ悪かったでしょう？
Kanji warukatta darō? ♂
感じ悪かっただろう？

I know I hurt your feelings.
Kizutsuketa-ne. ♂
傷付けたね。

I'll do anything to make you forgive me.
Yurushite-kureru-nara nandemo suru-wa. ♀
許してくれるなら何でもするわ。
Yurushite-kureru-nara nandemo suru-yo. ♂
許してくれるなら何でもするよ。

Anything?
Nandemo?
何でも？

I was blind to the truth.
Nani-ga hontō-kawakarana-katta.
何が本当か分からなかった。

You should understand how I feel.

Atashi-no kimochi mo kangaete. ♀
あたしの気持ちも考えて。

Boku-no kimochi mo kangaete. ♂
僕の気持ちも考えて。

You didn't even listen to me.

Kiite-mo kurenakatta.
聞いてもくれなかった。

Let's get back together.

Nakanaori-shiyō.
仲直りしよう。

Promise it will never happen again.

Mō okoranai-tte yakusoku-shite.
もう怒らないって約束して。

I promise.

Yakusoku-suru.
約束する。

Please take me back.

Yori-o modoshite.
よりを戻して。

Yori-o modosō-yo.
よりを戻そうよ。

I'm always doing silly things.

Atashi-tte itsumo baka-na-koto suru-yone. ♀
あたしっていつもばかな事
するよね。

Boku-tte itsumo baka-na-koto suru-yona. ♂
僕っていつもばかな事するよな。

I feel so lonely.

Samishii.
寂しい。.

I'm losing sleep.

Nemurenai-no. ♀
眠れないの。

Nemurenain-da. ♂
眠れないんだ。

You were the first and you'll be the last.

Anata-ga saisho-de, saigo-yo. ♀
あなたが最初で、最後よ。

Kimi-ga saisho-de, saigo-da. ♂
君が最初で、最後だ。

Whenever you need someone, I'll always be there.

Nani-ka attara, itsudemo itte.
何かあったら、いつでも言って。

Whatever you want I'll give it to you.

Nandemo hoshii mono ageru.
何でも欲しい物あげる。

Come back to me.

Atashi-no-moto-ni modotte-kite. ♀
あたしのもとに戻って来て。

Boku-no-moto-ni modotte-kite. ♂
僕のもとに戻って来て。

I believe you still love me.

Mada suki-tte shinjiteru.
まだ好きって信じてる。

Don't throw away this chance.

Kono chansu-o nogasanaide.
このチャンスを逃さないで。

It might be your last.

Saigo-kamo shirenai.
最後かもしれない。

Broken Intercourse

You forget everything.   *Anata-wa zembu wasurechau.* ♀
あなたは全部忘れちゃう。

Kimi-wa zembu wasureru. ♂
君は全部忘れる。

Have you forgotten so soon?   *Sonna-ni sugu wasurechatta-no?*
そんなにすぐ忘れちゃったの？

You forgot my birthday.   *Tanjōbi wasureteta deshō.* ♀
誕生日忘れてたでしょう。

Tanjōbi wasureteta darō. ♂
誕生日忘れてただろう。

You forgot our anniversary.   *Kinenbi wasureteta deshō.* ♀
記念日忘れてたでしょう。

Kinenbi wasureteta darō. ♂
記念日忘れてただろう。

Why didn't you call me?   *Nan-de denwa kurenakatta-no?*
何で電話くれなかったの？

I waited all night/a long time for your call.   *Hitoban-jū/Zutto denwa-o matteta.*
一晩中／ずっと電話を待ってた。

I was just about to call you.	***Anata-ni denwa-shiyō to omottetan-dakedo...*** ♀ あなたに電話しようと思ってたんだけど...。 ***Kimi-ni denwa-shiyō to omottetan-dakedo...*** ♂ 君に電話しようと思ってたんだけど...。
I tried to call you.	***Denwa-shita-noyo.*** ♀ 電話したのよ。 ***Denwa-shitan-dayo.*** ♂ 電話したんだよ。
I was busy.	***Isogashikatta.*** 忙しかった。
I didn't have ten yen.	***Jū-en-ga nakatta.*** 10円がなかった。

This is the cost of a short local call from a public phone—but as everyone has (or is expected to have) a mobile phone, this won't hold much water!

Why didn't you email me?	***Nan-de mēru kurenakatta-no?*** 何でメールくれなかったの？
I had no credit on my phone.	***Kozeni-ga nakatta.*** こぜにがなかった。
My (phone's) battery was flat.	***Batterii-ga kireta.*** バッテリーが切れた。
I was out of range.	***Dempa-ga yowakatta.*** 電波が弱かった。
Where were you?	***Doko-ni ita-no?*** どこにいたの？
That's a secret!	***Himitsu-yo!*** ♀ 秘密よ！ ***Himitsu-dayo!*** ♂ 秘密だよ！

Don't trick me/lie to me. *Uso tsukanaide.* ♀
嘘つかないで。

Uso tsukuna-yo. ♂
嘘つくなよ。

You lied to me. *Usotsuita-deshō.*
嘘ついたでしょう。

Usotsuita-darō. ♂
嘘ついただろう。

You lie to me all the time. *Itsumo uso-bakkari.*
いつも嘘ばっかり。

Stop lying to me. *Mō uso wa yamete!* ♀
もう嘘は止めて。

It was stupid of me to trust you. *Shinjita-atashi-ga baka-datta.* ♀
信じたあたしがばかだった。

Shinjita-boku-ga baka-datta. ♂
信じた僕がばかだった。

I can't trust you anymore. *Anata-no-koto mō shinjirare-nai.* ♀
あなたの事もう信じられない。

Kimi-no-koto mō shinjirare-nai. ♂
君の事もう信じられない。

Everything you've said is a lie.	*Anata-ga itta-koto zembu uso-jan.* ♀ あなたが言った事全部嘘じゃん。 *Kimi-ga itta-koto zembu uso-jan.* ♂ 君が言った事全部嘘じゃん。
So, what do you want me to say?	*Atashi-ni nante itte hoshii-no?* ♀ あたしに何て言って欲しいの？ *Boku-ni nante itte hoshiin-da?* ♂ 僕に何て言って欲しいんだ？
Let me speak frankly.	*Hontō-no-koto iwasete.* 本当の事言わせて。
I'm sorry, but...	*Warui-kedo,...* 悪いけど…。
Do you want to know the truth?	*Hontō-no-koto shiritai?* 本当の事知りたい？
What you say isn't important.	*Anata-ga iu-koto-wa taishita-koto janai-wa.* ♀ あなたが言う事は大した事じゃないわ。 *Kimi-ga iu-koto-wa taishita-koto janain-da.* ♀ 君が言う事は大した事じゃないんだ。
You're so selfish!	*Sugoi wagamama!* すごい我がまま！
Who am I to you?	*Atashi-wa anata-no nan-nano?* ♀ あたしはあなたの何なの？ *Boku-wa kimi-no nan-nanda?* ♂ 僕は君の何なんだ？

Who do you think I am?   *Atashi-o nanda-to omotteru-no?* ♀
あたしを何だと思ってるの?

Boku-o nanda-to omotterun-da? ♂
僕を何だと思ってるんだ?

I wasn't born yesterday.   *Sonna-ni baka-janai-yo.*
そんなにばかじゃないよ。

This literally means "I'm not a fool."

I don't belong here.   *Bachigai.*
場違い。

Don't pretend nothing happened.   *Nani-mo nakatta-yō-na kao-shinaide.* ♀
何もなかったような顔しないで。

Nani-mo nakatta-yō-na kao-suruna. ♂
何もなかったような顔するな。

How can you act like that (to me)?   *Dōshite sonna kao suru-no?* ♀
どうしてそんな顔するの?

Dōshite sonna kao surun-da? ♂
どうしてそんな顔するんだ?

You made me do it.   *Anata-ga sō saseta-no.* ♀
あなたがそうさせたの。

Kimi-ga sō sasetan-darō. ♂
君がそうさせたんだろう。

Don't make excuses.   *Iiwake-shinaide.* ♀
言い訳しないで。

Iiwake-suruna. ♂
言い訳するな。

Breaking Up! 13

You told me that you loved me, didn't you?

Suki-tte itta-jan?
好きって言ったじゃん？

Are you telling me you don't love me anymore?

Atashi-no koto mō suki janai-no? ♀
あたしの事もう好きじゃないの？

Boku-no koto mō suki janai-no? ♂
僕の事もう好きじゃないの？

I'm tired of you.

Anata-niwa akita. ♀
あなたには飽きた。

Kimi-niwa akita. ♂
君には飽きた。

Are you tired of me?

Atashi-ni akita-no? ♀
あたしに飽きたの？

Boku-ni akita-no? ♂
僕に飽きたの？

I knew it wouldn't work.

Dame-datte wakatteta.
だめだって分かってた。

Dame-datte wakatteta-yo. ♂
だめだって分かってたよ。

You've changed, haven't you?	**Nanka kawatta-nē?** 何か変わったねえ？
You messed up my life.	**Atashi-no jinsei mechakucha-ni shita.** ♀ あたしの人生めちゃくちゃにした。 **Boku-no jinsei mechakucha-ni shita.** ♂ 僕の人生めちゃくちゃにした。
Don't hurt me anymore.	**Mō kizutsukenaide.** もう傷つけないで。
Let's not tie each other up.	**Otagai-ni kanshō suru-no-wa yameyō.** お互いに干渉するのは止めよう。

This implies "Let's see other people."

You're the one who said, "Let's stop seeing each other."	**Anata-ga mō awanai-tte ittanjan?** ♀ あなたがもう会わないって言ったんじゃん？ **Kimi-ga mō awanai-tte ittanjan?** ♂ 君がもう会わないって言ったんじゃん？
You're using me/You take me for granted.	**Atashi-o riyō-shiteru-deshō?** ♀ あたしを利用してるでしょう？ **Boku-o riyō-shiteru-darō?** ♂ 僕を利用してるだろう？

This is a very strong accusation–don't use it lightly!

Do you know what you're doing?	**Dō-iu tsumori?** どういうつもり？ **Nani-sama-no tsumori?** 何様のつもり？
Don't tell me what to do.	**Urusaku-iwanaide.** うるさく言わないで。

I don't tell you what to do.

Urusaku-iwanai/ittenai-deshō. ♀
うるさく言わない／言ってない
　　でしょう。

Urusaku-iwanai/ittenai-darō. ♂
うるさく言わない／言ってない
　　だろう。

I'll do whatever I want.

Atashi-wa katte-ni suru-wa. ♀
あたしは勝手にするわ。

Boku-wa katte-ni suru-yo. ♂
僕は勝手にするよ。

Don't try to change me.

Atashi-o kaenaide. ♀
あたしを変えないで。

Boku-o kaenaide. ♂
僕を変えないで。

I can't be what you want me to be.

Anata-no risō-niwa narenai. ♀
あなたの理想にはなれない。

Kimi-no risō-niwa narenai. ♂
君の理想にはなれない。

Let me be me.

Atashi-no mama-de isasete. ♀
あたしのままでいさせて。

Boku-no mama-de isasete. ♂
僕のままでいさせて。

Leave me alone.

Hottoite.
ほっといて。

Stop following me around.

Tsuite-kuru-no-wa yamete.
付いて来るのは止めて。

Tsuite konaide.
付いて来ないで。

Tsuite kuruna! ♂
付いて来るな。

Stop checking up on me.

Atashi-no-koto kiku-no-wa yamete.
あたしの事聞くのは止めて。♀

***Boku-no-koto kiku-no-wa
   yamete.*** ♂
僕の事聞くのは止めて。

Stop troubling me.   ***Komarasenaide.***
困らせないで。

Don't embarrass me.   ***Haji kakasenaide.***
恥かかせないで。

Haji kakaseru-nayo. ♂
恥かかせるなよ。

Don't disappoint me   ***(Mō) gakkari-sasenaide.***
(again).   (もう)がっかりさせないで。

(Mō) gakkari-saseruna. ♂
(もう)がっかりさせるな。

I'm disappointed in you. ***Anata-niwa gakkari-shita.*** ♀
あなたにはがっかりした。

Kimi-niwa gakkari-shita. ♂
君にはがっかりした。

How many girls have you ***Ima-made nannin nakasete***
made cry?   ***kitano?*** ♀
今まで何人泣かせて来たの？

How many boys have you ***Ima-made nannin nakasete***
made cry?   ***kitanda?*** ♂
今まで何人泣かせて来たんだ？

Think about the way you acted/treated me!	*Anata-ga donna koto shita-ka kangaete mite-yo!* ♀ あなたがどんな事したか考えて みてよ！ *Kimi-ga donna koto shita-ka kangaete miro!* ♂ 君がどんな事したか考えてみろ！
Are you playing around with me?	*Atashi-no-koto asobi-nano?* ♀ あたしの事遊びなの？ *Boku-no-koto asobi-nano?* ♂ 僕の事遊びなの？

I didn't mean to.	*Sonna tsumori-ja nakatta.* そんなつもりじゃなかった。
It was just a game.	*Dōse asobi dattan-desho.* ♀ どうせ遊びだったんでしょ。 *Tada-no asobi-dattanda.* ♂ ただの遊びだったんだ。
Stop playing these games.	*Gomakasu-no-wa yamete-yo.* ♀ ごまかすのは止めてよ。 *Gomakasu-no-wa yamero-yo.* ♂ ごまかすのは止めろよ。

This means something like "Stop trying to hide the truth," "Don't change the subject," and "Stop acting like nothing happened" all rolled into one.

Stop nagging.	*Gocha-gocha iwanaide-yo (better for girls).* ごちゃごちゃ言わないでよ。 *Gata-gata iwanaide-yo.* ♀ がたがた言わないでよ。 *Gocha-gocha iuna.* ♂ ごちゃごちゃ言うな。 *Gata-gata iuna.* ♂ がたがた言うな。

With familiarity, some Japanese girls who were initially shy, might become possessive and demand to know your whereabouts all the time. You might need the following phrases.

We did it only once.	*Ikkai yatta dake-desho.* ♀ 1回やっただけでしょ。 *Ikkai yatta dake-darō.* ♂ 1回やっただけだろう。
Don't act like my husband!	*Teishu-zura shinaide!* ♀ 亭主づらしないで！
Don't act like my wife!	*Nyōbō-zura suruna!* ♂ 女房づらするな！
Don't act like I'm yours.	*Wagamono-gao shinaide.* ♀ 我が物顔しないで。 *Wagamono-gao suruna.* ♂ 我が物顔するな。
Go look in the mirror!	*Kagami mite kina-yo!* ♀ 鏡見てきなよ！ *Kagami mite koi-yo!* ♂ 鏡見てこいよ！

I've had it!

Mō takusan!
もうたくさん！

For extra emphasis stop abruptly on the "n."

I need excitement, not restriction.

Shigeki-ga hoshii-no, sokubaku-sarerun-janakutte. ♀
刺激が欲しいの、束縛されるん
じゃなくって。

Shigeki-ga hoshiin-da, sokubaku-sarerun-janakutte. ♂
刺激が欲しいんだ、束縛されるん
じゃなくって。

You don't excite me anymore.

Anata-niwa mō shigeki-ga nai-no. ♀
あなたにはもう刺激がないの。

Anata-niwa mō dokidoki shinai-no. ♀
あなたにはもうどきどきしないの。

Kimi-niwa mō shigeki-ga nain-da. ♂
君にはもう刺激がないんだ。

Kimi-niwa mō dokidoki shinai. ♂
君にはもうどきどきしない。

You aren't any good in bed.

Hetakuso!
下手くそ！

Hetakuso! has a broad meaning of "you're no good!" To make yourself completely clear, use it when pointing at the person.

You mean nothing (to me).

Anata-no sonzai-wa muimi. ♀
あなたの存在は無意味。

Kimi-no sonzai-wa muimi. ♂
君の存在は無意味。

I'm glad we broke up.

Wakarete yokkatta.
別れてよかった。

(Pack your stuff and) hit the road!	***Mō dete-itte!*** もう出て行って！

Give me back the apartment/car key.	***Apāto/kuruma-no kagi-o kaeshite-yo.*** ♀ アパート／車のかぎを返してよ。 ***Apāto/kuruma-no kagi-o kaese-yo.*** ♂ アパート／車のかぎを返せよ。
Give me back all the presents I gave to you.	***Atashi-ga ageta mono zembu kaeshite-yo.*** ♀ あたしがあげた物全部返してよ。 ***Boku-ga ageta mono zembu kaese-yo.*** ♂ 僕があげた物全部返せよ。
I've already thrown them away.	***Mō suteta(wa)-yo.*** ♀ もう捨てた(わ)よ。 ***Mō suteta-yo.*** もう捨てたよ。
Why did you do such a thing?	***Nande sonna-koto shita-no?*** ♀ 何でそんな事したの？ ***Nande sonna-koto shitan-dayo?*** ♂ 何でそんな事したんだよ？
(Because) I wanted to forget you.	***Anata-o wasuretakatta (kara).*** ♀ あなたを忘れたかった(から)。 ***Kimi-o wasuretakatta (kara).*** ♂ 君を忘れたかった(から)。
Don't do such a thing.	***Sonna-koto shinaide.*** そんな事しないで。

(You're such a) worrier.

Shimpaishō.
心配性。

(You're such a) crybaby.

Nakimushi.
泣きむし。

I'm not your toy.

Atashi-wa omocha-janai. ♀
あたしはおもちゃじゃない。

Boku-wa omocha-janai. ♂
僕はおもちゃじゃない。

Don't think that I'm only yours.

Atashi-wa anata-dake-no mono janai-wayo. ♀
あたしはあなただけの物じゃないわよ。

Boku-wa kimi-dake-no mono janai-yo. ♂
僕は君だけの物じゃないよ。

I don't belong to you.

Atashi-wa anata-no kanojo janai. ♀
あたしはあなたの彼女じゃない。

Boku-wa kimi-no kareshi janai. ♂
僕は君の彼氏じゃない。

Now I'll feel better (because we broke up).

Kore-de sukkiri-shita.
これですっきりした。

Literally means "I'm refreshed because of what happened."

You said bad things about me.

Atashi-no waruguchi itta-deshō? ♀
あたしの悪口言ったでしょう？

Boku-no waruguchi itta-darō? ♂
僕の悪口言っただろう？

How can you talk (to me) like that?

Nande sonna-fū-ni ieru-no? ♀
何でそんなふうに言えるの？

Nande sonna-fū-ni ierun-dayo. ♂
何でそんなふうに言えるんだよ？

You talk down to me.

Mikudashiterun-deshō? ♀
見下してるんでしょう？
Mikudashiterun-darō? ♂
見下してるんだろう？

You talk to me like I'm a fool.

Baka-dato omotteru deshō? ♀
ばかだと思ってるでしょう？
Baka-dato omotteru darō? ♂
ばかだと思ってるだろう？

Who cares?

Dare-ga sonna-koto ki-ni suru-noyo? ♀
誰がそんな事気にするのよ？
Dare-ga sonna-koto ki-ni surun-dayo? ♂
誰がそんな事気にするんだよ？

I hate you!

Anata/Anta-nante kirai! ♀
あなた／あんたなんて嫌い！
Omae-nante kirai-dayo! ♂
お前なんて嫌いだよ！

I can find someone better than you.

Anata-yori ii hito-nante takusan iru-wa. ♀
あなたよりいい人なんてたくさん
いるわ。
Kimi-yori ii ko-nante takusan iru-yo. ♂
君よりいい子なんてたくさんいる
よ。

Who would want you?

Dare-ga anata/anta-to tsukiau-noyo? ♀
誰があなた／あんたと付き合う
のよ？
Dare-ga kimi/omae-to tsukiaun-dayo? ♂
誰が君／お前と付き合うんだよ？

You're not the only
boy in this world.

*Anata/Anta-no hoka-ni-mo
otoko nante takusan
iru-wayo.* ♀
あなた/あんたの他にも男なんて
たくさんいるわよ。

You're not the only
girl in this would.

*Kimi/Omae-no hoka-ni-mo onna
nante takusan irun-dayo.* ♂
君/お前の他にも女なんて
たくさんいるんだよ。

You can't find anyone
better than me.

*Atashi-yori ii-onna-ga iru-to
omotteru-no?* ♀
あたしよりいい女がいると思って
るの?

*Boku-ijō-no-yatsu-ga iru-to
omotteru-no-ka?* ♂
僕よりいい男がいると思ってる
のか?

I can see whomever I
want/do whatever
I want.

*Atashi-wa yaritai yō-ni
suru-wa.* ♀
あたしはやりたいようにするわ。
*Boku-wa yaritai yō-ni
suru-yo.* ♂
僕はやりたいようにするよ。

Do it!

Sure-ba!
すれば!
Shiro-yo! ♂
しろよ!

Go find yourself a new boyfriend/girlfriend.

Atarashii kanojo-o sagaseba. ♀
新しい彼女を探せば。

Atarashii kareshi-o sagase-yo. ♂
新しい彼氏を探せよ。

I've been lying to you/ cheated on you.

Uso tsuiteta.
嘘ついてた。

Damashiteta.
だましてた。

I don't want to believe that.

Shinjitakunai.
信じたくない。

Cheater/Two-timer!

Uwaki-mono!
浮気者。

Uwaki-mono literally means "floating mind," and is usually combined with other insults, such as...

You're the worst!

Saitei!
最低！

Saiaku!
最悪！

I have another boyfriend/ girlfriend.

Hoka-ni kareshi-ga iru-no. ♀
他に彼氏がいるの。

Hoka-ni kanojo-ga irun-da. ♂
他に彼女がいるんだ。

I've tried to tell you manytimes, but I couldn't.

Nankai-mo iō-to shitanda-kedo.
何回も言おうとしたんだけど。

I know you're seeing someone else.

Futamata kaketeru-deshō? ♀
二またかけてるでしょう？
Futamata kaketeru-darō? ♂
二またかけてるだろう？

I know how you look at other girls.

Donna-fū-ni hoka-no-ko-no koto kangaeteru-ka shitteru-wa. ♀
どんなふうに他の子の事考えてるか知ってるわ。

I know how you look at other boys.

Donna-fū-ni hoka-no-otoko-no koto kangaeteru-ka shitteru-yo. ♂
どんなふうに他の男の事考えてるか知ってるよ。

I saw you with another girl.

Anata/Anta-ga onna-to iru-no-o mita-wa. ♀
あなた／あんたが女といるのを見たわ。

I saw you with another boy.

Kimi/Omae-ga-otoko-to iru-no-o mita-yo. ♂
君／お前が男といるのを見たよ。

What kind of girl/boy is she/he?

Ano ko dare?
あの子誰？
Ano hito dare?
あの人誰？

You'd better believe that.

Shinjite-yo. ♀
信じてよ。
Shinjite-kureyo. ♂
信じてくれよ。

I believed in you, yet you tricked me.

Shinjiteta-noni damashita deshō. ♀
信じてたのにだましたでしょう。
Shinjiteta-noni damashita darō. ♂
信じてたのにだましただろう。

Choose: her/him or me.

Docchi-ga suki-nano?
どっちが好きなの？

Docchi-ni suru-no?
どっちにするの

I won't forgive you.

Anata-o yurusanai. ♀
あなたを許さない。

Kimi-o yurusanai. ♂
君を許さない。

Be nice to your new
sweetheart.

*Atarashii kanojo-to nakayoku-
ne.* ♀
新しい彼女と仲良くね。

*Atarashii kareshi-to nakayoku-
na.* ♂
新しい彼氏と仲良くな。

Don't make her/him sad.

*Kanojo/Kareshi-o nakasecha
dame-dayo.*
彼女／彼氏を泣かせちゃだめだよ。

Have you already decided
(which one)?

Mō kimeta?
もう決めた？

Don't make promises
you can't keep.

*Mamorenai yakusoku-wa
shinaide.*
守れない約束はしないで。

I can't stand it.

Mō taerarenai.
もうたえられない。

It happens all the time.

Itsumo sō naru.
いつもそうなる。

You never came over.

Konakatta deshō. ♀
来なかったでしょう。

Konakatta darō. ♂
来なかっただろう。

You left me (stranded)
(at...).

(...-ni) oitetta deshō. ♀
(…に) おいてったでしょう。

(...-ni) oitetta darō. ♂
(…に) おいてっただろう。

You left without telling me.	***Nani-mo iwanaide itchatta.*** 何も言わないで行っちゃった。
I can't give her/him up.	***(Moto kanojo/kareshi-o)*** ***akiramerarenai.*** （元彼女／彼氏を）諦められない。
I can't forget her/him.	***(Moto kanojo/kareshi-o)*** ***wasure-rarenai.*** （元彼女／彼氏を）忘れられない。
I can't forgive her/him.	***(Moto kanojo/kareshi-o)*** ***yuruse-nai.*** （元彼女／彼氏を）許せない。